Effortless Asian Recipe

Thai Delights, Filipino Fare,
Indonesian Dishes, Korean and
Vietnamese Cuisine

Boniface Johnson

Table of Contents

CHAPTER 1: KOREAN RECIPES
EASY KOREAN COOKBOOK

SPICY TOFU SALAD

Ingredients

- 3 green onions, chopped
- two tbsps. soy sauce
- two tbsps. toasted sesame seeds

- one half tsps. Korean chili pepper powder, or to taste
- one tsp. white sugar
- half tsp. toasted Asian sesame oil
- one half cups steamed Japanese rice
- half head of romaine lettuce (heart only), torn into bite-size pieces
- half cucumber - peeled, seeded, and chopped
- one (1two ounce) package tofu, sliced

Directions

- Combine green onions, sesame seeds, Korean red pepper powder, soy sauce, sugar, and sesame oil in a regular sized bowl thoroughly
- Now put the rice in bowl and add a mixture of lettuce and cucumber before putting tofu over it.
- Now pour some sesame mixture over the tofu according to your tastes.

Serving: one large bowl

Timing Information:

Preparation	Cooking	Total Time
10 mins		10 mins

Nutritional Information:

Calories	198 kcal
Carbohydrates	23.7 g
Cholesterol	0 mg
Fat	7.2 g
Fiber	1.9 g
Protein	10.4 g
Sodium	472 mg

* Percent Daily Values are based on a 2,000 calorie diet.

Kimchee Squats

Ingredients

- two lbs. chopped Chinese cabbage
- one tbsp. salt
- two tbsps. chopped green onion
- one clove garlic, crushed
- one tbsp. chili powder
- two tsps. minced fresh ginger root
- half cup light soy sauce
- half cup white wine vinegar
- two tsps. white sugar
- one dash sesame oil

Directions

- Let cabbage sit for 4 hours after adding some salt and massage it with your hands until you find that it is soft.
- Now drain all the liquid and add green onion, soy sauce, sugar, ginger, garlic and chili powder into this cabbage.
- Refrigerate for about 24 hours in a jar before serving.

Serving: 6

Timing Information:

Preparation	Cooking	Total Time
25 mins	10 mins	1 day 4 hrs 25 min

Nutritional Information:

Calories	36 kcal
Carbohydrates	**6.8 g**
Cholesterol	0 mg
Fat	**0.5 g**
Fiber	**1.9 g**
Protein	**2.6 g**
Sodium	1796 mg

* Percent Daily Values are based on a 2,000 calorie diet.

CARROT SALAD

Ingredients

- one lb. carrots, peeled and julienned (preferably with a mandolin)
- three cloves garlic, minced
- 1/4 cup vinegar
- one tbsp. white sugar
- two half tsps. salt
- 1/three cup vegetable oil
- half onion, minced
- one tsp. ground coriander
- half tsp. cayenne pepper

Directions

- Add garlic over carrots in a bowl and separately mix vinegar, sugar, and salt thoroughly.
- Cook onions in hot oil for about 5 minutes and add coriander and cayenne pepper before adding everything to the carrot mixture.
- Also add vinegar dressing over the mixture and refrigerate in a sealed dish for about 24 hours while tossing it several times.

Serving: 6

Timing Information:

Preparation	Cooking	Total Time
30 mins	10 mins	1 hrs 30 mins

Nutritional Information:

Calories	119 kcal
Carbohydrates	8.9 g
Cholesterol	0 mg
Fat	9.3 g
Fiber	2 g
Protein	0.8 g
Sodium	767 mg

* Percent Daily Values are based on a 2,000 calorie diet.

Spicy Red Pepper Cucumbers

Ingredients

- one tsp. vegetable oil
- two tbsps. sesame seeds
- two tbsps. kochujang (Korean hot sauce)
- 1/4 cup white vinegar
- one tbsp. sesame oil
- 1 green onion, chopped
- one cucumber, halved, seeded and thinly sliced

Directions

- Place sesame seeds in a large bowl after cooking in hot vegetable oil for about three minutes and add kochujang, green onion and sesame oil into the sesame seeds.
- Now add cucumber and mix well.
- Serve.

Serving: two cups

Timing Information:

Preparation	Cooking	Total Time
10 mins	5 mins	15 mins

Nutritional Information:

Calories	1092 kcal
Carbohydrates	57.5 g
Cholesterol	155 mg
Fat	78.6 g
Fiber	1.8 g
Protein	39.1 g
Sodium	2501 mg

* Percent Daily Values are based on a 2,000 calorie diet.

Salad with Sesame Dressing

Ingredients

- one head red leaf lettuce
- 4 green onions (white part only)
- 1/4 cup soy sauce
- 5 tbsps. water
- two tsps. white sugar
- 1/4 cup distilled white vinegar
- two tbsps. sesame oil
- one tbsp. red pepper flakes

Directions

- Place lettuce leaves into a bowl after washing and cutting.
- Now add the sliced white portion of your sliced green onions into the bowl containing the lettuce leaves.
- In a separate bowl mix soy sauce, white sugar, vinegar, sesame oil, water, and red pepper flakes and pour this mixture over the bowl containing lettuce leaves and green onions.
- Serve.

Serving: 5 cups

Timing Information:

Preparation	Cooking	Total Time
10 mins		10 mins

Nutritional Information:

Calories	80 kcal
Carbohydrates	6.1 g
Cholesterol	0 mg
Fat	5.9 g
Fiber	1.6 g
Protein	2 g
Sodium	740 mg

* Percent Daily Values are based on a 2,000 calorie diet.

Korean Cucumber Salad

Ingredients

- three lbs. seedless cucumber, sliced paper-thin
- one half tbsps. sea salt
- half cup rice vinegar
- one tbsp. rice wine
- two tbsps. sesame oil
- two tbsps. honey
- two tbsps. freshly squeezed lemon juice
- 1 green onion, sliced
- one tbsp. toasted sesame seeds
- two walnut halves, finely chopped(optional)
- one clove garlic, minced
- one half tsps. Korean red pepper powder
- freshly ground black pepper to taste

Directions

- Drain liquid from cucumbers after putting some sea salt by letting it stand for about 15 minutes and wrapping it in a paper towel to get more water out of it.
- Now combine rice vinegar, rice wine, honey, green onion, sesame seeds, lemon juice, walnuts, garlic, sesame oil, Korean red pepper powder and ground black pepper in a medium sized bowl.
- In this mixture, add cucumbers and refrigerate for at least 30 minutes after wrapping with plastic paper.

Serving: 10

Timing Information:

Preparation	Cooking	Total Time
10 mins		40 mins

Nutritional Information:

Calories	117 kcal
Carbohydrates	**15.8 g**
Cholesterol	0 mg
Fat	**6.1 g**
Fiber	**1.7 g**
Protein	**2.1 g**
Sodium	1332 mg

* Percent Daily Values are based on a 2,000 calorie diet.

KIMCHEE JUN

(KIMCHEE PANCAKES)

Ingredients
- one cup kimchi, drained and chopped
- half cup reserved juice from kimchi
- one cup all-purpose flour
- two eggs
- 1 green onion, chopped
- one tbsp. vegetable oil
- salt to taste
- one tbsp. rice vinegar
- one tbsp. soy sauce
- half tsp. sesame oil
- half tsp. Korean chili pepper flakes (optional)
- half tsp. toasted sesame seeds (optional)

Directions
- Combine kimchi, flour, eggs, kimchi juice and green onion in a medium sized bowl.
- Cook pancakes made from ¼ cup of batter in hot vegetable oil for about 5 minutes each side.
- Now combine rice vinegar, sesame oil, chili pepper flakes, soy sauce and toasted sesame seeds in a bowl and serve this with pancakes.

Serving: 8 cups

Timing Information:

Preparation	Cooking	Total Time
15 mins	15 mins	30 mins

Nutritional Information:

Calories	199 kcal
Carbohydrates	26.5 g
Cholesterol	93 mg
Fat	7.1 g
Fiber	1.6 g
Protein	7.4 g
Sodium	513 mg

* Percent Daily Values are based on a 2,000 calorie diet.

Jap Chae

(Glass Noodles)

Ingredients

- one pkg. (8 serving size) sweet potato vermicelli
- half cup reduced-sodium soy sauce
- 1/4 cup brown sugar
- half cup boiling water
- three tbsps. vegetable oil
- one tsp. toasted sesame seeds

Directions

- Cover the vermicelli with hot water after cutting it into small pieces for 10 minutes and add a mixture of soy sauce, boiling water, and brown sugar into it.
- Cook this mixture in hot oil for about 5 minutes and just before serving, add noodles over it.

Serving: 4

Timing Information:

Preparation	Cooking	Total Time
15 mins	5 mins	20 mins

Nutritional Information:

Calories	363 kcal
Carbohydrates	65.2 g
Cholesterol	0 mg
Fat	10.7 g
Fiber	0.6 g
Protein	1.9 g
Sodium	1073 mg

* Percent Daily Values are based on a 2,000 calorie diet.

Kongnamool

(Soybean Sprouts)

Ingredients

- one lb. soybean sprouts
- two tbsps. soy sauce
- 1/4 cup sesame oil
- two tbsps. Korean chili powder
- one half tsps. garlic, minced
- two tsps. sesame seeds
- 1/4 cup chopped green onion
- two tsps. rice wine vinegar, or to taste

Directions

- Cook bean sprouts in salty boiling water for about 15 seconds and drain the water.
- Put sprouts in ice cold water for about three minutes to stop the cooking process and when these bean sprouts are cold, set them aside.
- Now combine soy sauce, sesame seeds, sesame oil and chili powder in a medium sized bowl and add bean sprouts to it.
- Now add some green onion and rice wine vinegar before refrigerating for some time.
- Serve

Serving: 4

Timing Information:

Preparation	Cooking	Total Time
10 mins	5 mins	15 mins

Nutritional Information:

Calories	376 kcal
Carbohydrates	21.4 g
Cholesterol	69 mg
Fat	21.9 g
Fiber	0.8 g
Protein	20.6 g
Sodium	1249 mg

* Percent Daily Values are based on a 2,000 calorie diet.

Zucchini In Korea

Ingredients

- 5 medium zucchini, sliced
- one bunch green onions, sliced
- 1/4 cup white vinegar
- half cup soy sauce
- 1/4 cup water
- two tbsps. sugar
- two tbsps. sesame oil
- ground black pepper to taste

Directions

- Mix zucchini, vinegar, soy sauce, water, sugar, green onions and sesame oil in a saucepan before adding pepper and cooking for about 20 minutes to get the zucchini tender.

Serving: 6

Timing Information:

Preparation	Cooking	Total Time
20 mins	20 mins	40 mins

Nutritional Information:

Calories	1092 kcal
Carbohydrates	57.5 g
Cholesterol	155 mg
Fat	78.6 g
Fiber	1.8 g
Protein	39.1 g
Sodium	2501 mg

* Percent Daily Values are based on a 2,000 calorie diet.

RED PEPPER POTATOES

Ingredients

- one half tbsps. soy sauce
- one pinch cayenne pepper, or to taste
- one half tbsps. vegetable oil
- three potatoes, cut into bite sized pieces
- 4 green onions, chopped
- one large red bell pepper, chopped
- two tsps. sesame seeds

Directions

- Mix cayenne pepper and soy sauce in a bowl and cook potatoes over hot vegetable oil for about 5 minutes or until golden.
- Continue to cook for another minute after adding onion bell pepper and sesame seeds.
- Add soy sauce mixture and cook for another 3 minutes.

Serving: 4

Timing Information:

Preparation	Cooking	Total Time
15 mins	20 mins	35 mins

Nutritional Information:

Calories	198 kcal
Carbohydrates	32.3 g
Cholesterol	0 mg
Fat	6.2 g
Fiber	5 g
Protein	4.6
Sodium	352 mg

* Percent Daily Values are based on a 2,000 calorie diet.

FIDDLEHEADS

Ingredients

- three cups fresh fiddlehead ferns, ends trimmed
- three tbsps. unfiltered extra-virgin olive oil
- one clove garlic, minced
- half tsp. sea salt
- half tsp. black pepper
- one tbsp. fresh lemon juice

Directions

- Cook fiddlehead ferns in salty boiling water for about 10 minutes and drain the water.
- Add pepper, and garlic in some hot olive oil along with the ferns for about 5 minutes and remove everything from the heat and add lemon juice before serving.

Serving: 3

Timing Information:

Preparation	Cooking	Total Time
15 mins	15 mins	30 mins

Nutritional Information:

Calories	376 kcal
Carbohydrates	21.4 g
Cholesterol	69 mg
Fat	21.9 g
Fiber	0.8 g
Protein	20.6 g
Sodium	1249 mg

* Percent Daily Values are based on a 2,000 calorie diet.

CRAB CAKES IN KOREA

Ingredients

- 1/4 cup mayonnaise
- two tbsps. chopped fresh cilantro
- one tbsp. chopped fresh ginger
- two tsps. Asian fish sauce (nuoc mam or nam pla)
- one (6 ounce) can crabmeat - drained, flaked and cartilage removed
- three ounces chopped shrimp
- one half cups fresh breadcrumbs, made from crustless French bread
- salt and pepper to taste
- one half tbsps. peanut oil

Directions

- Combine crab, shrimp, bread crumbs, fresh ginger, mayonnaise, fish sauce and cilantro together in a bowl before adding salt and pepper.
- Take one fourth of a cup of this mixture and place in a bowl containing the remaining bread crumbs, and make a patty out of it.
- Do the same for the rest of the crab mixture.
- Now fry your patties in in hot oil over medium heat for about 5 minutes each side.
- Serve

Serving: 4

Timing Information:

Preparation	Cooking	Total Time
15 mins	35 mins	50 mins

Nutritional Information:

Calories	254 kcal
Carbohydrates	9.6 g
Cholesterol	75 mg
Fat	17.4 g
Fiber	0.5 g
Protein	14.5 g
Sodium	620 mg

* Percent Daily Values are based on a 2,000 calorie diet.

Corn and Cashew Hummus

Ingredients

- two cups corn kernels, thawed if frozen
- one cup cashews
- one tsp. lemon juice, or more to taste
- 1/4 tsp. salt
- 1/4 tsp. onion powder
- 1/4 tsp. garlic powder

Directions

- Place everything mentioned in a blender and blend it for about one minute.
- Serve with rice.

Serving: 3

Timing Information:

Preparation	Cooking	Total Time
5 mins		5 mins

Nutritional Information:

Calories	270 kcal
Carbohydrates	28.6 g
Cholesterol	0 mg
Fat	16.5 g
Fiber	3 g
Protein	7.8 g
Sodium	367 mg

* Percent Daily Values are based on a 2,000 calorie diet.

Toasti

Ingredients

- half cup shredded cabbage
- half carrot, shredded
- one egg
- half tsp. soy sauce
- two tbsps. butter
- two slices bread, toasted

Directions

- Add egg and soy sauce into a mixture of cabbage and carrot, and mix thoroughly.
- Cook the patty made from this vegetable mixture in hot butter for about three minutes each side.
- Serve by placing contents between two slices of bread.

Serving: 1

Timing Information:

Preparation	Cooking	Total Time
10 mins	10 mins	20 mins

Nutritional Information:

Calories	431 kcal
Carbohydrates	30.9 g
Cholesterol	247 mg
Fat	29.8 g
Fiber	3 g
Protein	11.2 g
Sodium	751 mg

* Percent Daily Values are based on a 2,000 calorie diet.

Banana Waffles

Ingredients

- one 1/4 cups all-purpose flour
- three tsps. baking powder
- half tsp. salt
- one pinch ground nutmeg
- one cup 2% milk
- one egg
- two ripe bananas, sliced

Directions

- Combine nutmeg, baking powder, flour and salt and add milk and eggs.
- Pour two tbsps. of batter over preheated waffle iron after spraying the iron with non-stick cooking spray.
- Now place two slices of banana on the mixture pour another two tsps. of batter over these slices of banana.
- Cook for about three minutes or until golden brown.
- Serve

Serving: 4

Timing Information:

Preparation	Cooking	Total Time
10 mins	30 mins	40 mins

Nutritional Information:

Calories	241 kcal
Carbohydrates	47.3 g
Cholesterol	50 mg
Fat	2.5 g
Fiber	2.6 g
Protein	8.3 g
Sodium	606 mg

* Percent Daily Values are based on a 2,000 calorie diet.

EGGS KIMCHI

Ingredients

- two tbsps. vegetable oil
- one cup kimchi, or to taste
- two large eggs, beaten

Directions

- Cook kimchi in hot oil over medium heat for about two minutes and add eggs, and cook for another three minutes to get the eggs tender.
- Serve.

Serving: 4

Timing Information:

Preparation	Cooking	Total Time
5 mins	5 mins	10 mins

Nutritional Information:

Calories	208 kcal
Carbohydrates	3.5 g
Cholesterol	186 mg
Fat	18.8 g
Fiber	0.9 g
Protein	7.5 g
Sodium	568 mg

* Percent Daily Values are based on a 2,000 calorie diet.

Seaweed Soup

Ingredients

- one (one ounce) package dried brown seaweed
- 1/4 lb. beef top sirloin, minced
- two tsps. sesame oil
- one half tbsps. soy sauce
- one tsp. salt, or to taste
- 6 cups water
- one tsp. minced garlic

Directions

- Cover seaweed with water to get them soft and cut them into two inch pieces.
- Cook beef, half tbsp. of soy sauce and some salt for about one minute in a saucepan over medium heat.
- Now add seaweed and the remaining soy sauce and cook for another minute while stirring continuously.
- Bring to boil after adding two cups of water and add garlic and the remaining water.
- Cook this for 20 minutes and add salt before serving.

Serving: 4

Timing Information:

Preparation	Cooking	Total Time
15 mins	30 mins	45 mins

Nutritional Information:

Calories	65 kcal
Carbohydrates	1 g
Cholesterol	17 mg
Fat	3.7 g
Fiber	0.1 g
Protein	6.8 g
Sodium	940 mg

* Percent Daily Values are based on a 2,000 calorie diet.

KIMCHEE JIGEH

(STEW)

Ingredients

- 6 cups water
- three cups napa cabbage Kim Chee, brine reserved
- two cups cubed fully cooked luncheon meat (e.g. Spam)
- three tbsps. chili powder
- salt, to taste
- ground black pepper, to taste

Directions

- Take a large saucepan and combine water, kim chee, spam, pepper, chili powder, kim chee brine and salt.
- Bring this mixture to boil and cook for about 20 minutes.
- Serve.

Serving: 4

Timing Information:

Preparation	Cooking	Total Time
5 mins	20 mins	25 mins

Nutritional Information:

Calories	303 kcal
Carbohydrates	10.6 g
Cholesterol	59 mg
Fat	24.1 g
Fiber	3.5 g
Protein	13.7 g
Sodium	2064 mg

* Percent Daily Values are based on a 2,000 calorie diet.

MISO

(BEAN CURD SOUP)

Ingredients

- three half cups water
- three tbsps. denjang (Korean bean curd paste)
- one tbsp. garlic paste
- half tbsp. dashi granules
- half tbsp. gochujang (Korean hot pepper paste)
- one zucchini, cubed
- one potato, peeled and cubed
- 1/4 lb. fresh mushrooms, quartered
- one onion, chopped
- one (1two ounce) package soft tofu, sliced

Directions

- Combine water, denjang, garlic paste, dashi and gochujang in saucepan over medium heat and let it boil for two minutes.
- Now add zucchini, potato, onions and mushrooms, and cook for another 7 minutes.
- Now add tofu and cook until tender.

Serving: 4

Timing Information:

Preparation	Cooking	Total Time
15 mins	20 mins	35 mins

Nutritional Information:

Calories	158 kcal
Carbohydrates	21.6 g
Cholesterol	0 mg
Fat	4.1 g
Fiber	3.4 g
Protein	9.1 g
Sodium	641 mg

* Percent Daily Values are based on a 2,000 calorie diet.

DOENJANG CHIGAE

(BEAN TOFU SOUP)

Ingredients

- three cups vegetable stock
- three cups water
- two cloves garlic, coarsely chopped
- two tbsps. Korean soy bean paste (doenjang)
- 4 green onions, chopped
- one zucchini, halved and cut into 1/2-inch slices
- half (16 ounce) package firm tofu, drained and cubed
- one jalapeno pepper, sliced

Directions

- Add garlic and soy bean paste into boiled vegetable stock stirring regularly to dissolve.
- Now add green onion, tofu, jalapeno and zucchini, and cook for 15 minutes at low heat.
- Serve.

Serving: 6

Timing Information:

Preparation	Cooking	Total Time
15 mins	25 mins	40 mins

Nutritional Information:

Calories	59 kcal
Carbohydrates	5 g
Cholesterol	0 mg
Fat	2.7 g
Fiber	1.6 g
Protein	4.9 g
Sodium	378 mg

* Percent Daily Values are based on a 2,000 calorie diet.

Pine Nut Rice Soup

Ingredients

- one cup pine nuts
- two cups cooked long-grain white rice
- 6 cups water
- one tbsp. pine nuts
- one cup dates, pitted and chopped
- half tsp. white sugar
- salt to taste

Directions

- Blend rice, one cup pine nuts, and 2 glass of water in a blender.
- Add 4 cups of water and this pine nut mixture into saucepan, and bring it to boil.
- Cook for 10 minutes at low heat while stirring regularly to prevent it from burning.
- Garnish with sliced dates and more pine nuts.
- Serve.

Serving: 6

Timing Information:

Preparation	Cooking	Total Time
10 mins	10 mins	20 mins

Nutritional Information:

Calories	275 kcal
Carbohydrates	37 g
Cholesterol	0 mg
Fat	12.5 g
Fiber	3.3 g
Protein	7.8 g
Sodium	2 mg

* Percent Daily Values are based on a 2,000 calorie diet.

Shrimp Rice Soup

Ingredients

- two cups white rice
- 9 ounces shelled and deveined shrimp
- one tbsp. sesame oil
- one tbsp. rice wine
- 12 cups water
- salt to taste

Directions

- Let the rice stand for about two hours after rinsing it.
- Fry shrimp and rice wine in hot oil in a saucepan over medium heat and add rice cook for one minute.
- Pour some water into the saucepan and when the mixture is thick, turn the heat down to low and cook for another 10-15 minutes.
- Serve.

Serving: 4

Timing Information:

Preparation	Cooking	Total Time
2 hrs	20 mins	2 hrs 20 mins

Nutritional Information:

Calories	586 kcal
Carbohydrates	99.6 g
Cholesterol	128 mg
Fat	6.8 g
Fiber	1.6 g
Protein	25.9 g
Sodium	131 mg

* Percent Daily Values are based on a 2,000 calorie diet.

Seaweed Soup II

Ingredients

- one ounce dried wakame (brown) seaweed
- two tsps. sesame oil
- half cup extra-lean ground beef
- one tsp. salt, or to taste
- one half tbsps. soy sauce
- one tsp. minced garlic
- 7 cups water

Directions

- Let the seaweed stand in water for about 15 minutes to get soft, drain the water, and cut it into two inch pieces.
- Cook beef, 1/3 cup soy sauce and add some salt in hot oil in a saucepan over medium heat for about 4 minutes and add seaweed and the soy sauce that is left.
- Cook for another minute and add garlic and some water.
- Bring water to boil and lower the heat down to low and cook for another 15 minutes.
- Serve.

Serving: 4

Timing Information:

Preparation	Cooking	Total Time
10 mins	20 mins	40 mins

Nutritional Information:

Calories	376 kcal
Carbohydrates	21.4 g
Cholesterol	69 mg
Fat	21.9 g
Fiber	0.8 g
Protein	20.6 g
Sodium	1249 mg

* Percent Daily Values are based on a 2,000 calorie diet.

STEAK IN KOREA

Ingredients

- two lbs. thinly sliced Scotch fillet (chuck eye steaks)
- half cup soy sauce
- 5 tbsps. white sugar
- two half tbsps. sesame seeds
- two tbsps. sesame oil
- three shallots, thinly sliced
- two cloves garlic, crushed
- 5 tbsps. mirin (Japanese sweet wine)

Directions

- Combine soy sauce, sugar, sesame seeds, sesame oil, shallots, garlic, and mirin in a bowl before adding meat and mixing it thoroughly.
- Refrigerate for about 18 hours and fry this meat over hot oil for 10 minutes.
- Serve this meat with fried rice or salad.

Serving: 6

Timing Information:

Preparation	Cooking	Total Time
20 mins	10 mins	12 hrs 30 mins

Nutritional Information:

Calories	376 kcal
Carbohydrates	21.4 g
Cholesterol	69 mg
Fat	21.9 g
Fiber	0.8 g
Protein	20.6 g
Sodium	1249 mg

* Percent Daily Values are based on a 2,000 calorie diet.

CHAPTER 2: FILIPINO RECIPES
EASY FILIPINO COOKBOOK

FILIPINO OXTAIL STEW

Ingredients:

- 1 1/2 pounds beef oxtail, cut into pieces
- 1 large onion, quartered
- 2 cloves garlic, chopped
- 1 tsp salt
- 1/2 tsp ground black pepper, or to taste
- 1 large eggplant, cut into 2-inch chunks
- 1/2 head bok choy, cut into 1-inch pieces

- 1/2 pound fresh green beans, trimmed and snapped into 2-inch pieces
- 1/4 cup peanut butter, or as needed to thicken sauce

Directions:

- Bring the mixture of oxtail pieces, pepper, garlic and salt to boil in water before cooking it for two hours over medium heat.
- Now add eggplant, green beans and bok choy into this mixture before cooking it for another 20 minutes or until the vegetables you just added are tender.
- Add a mixture of peanut butter and some broth into the stew just before you serve it.

•

Serving: 6

Timing Information:

Preparation	Cooking	Total Time
2 hr 20 mins	2 hr 20 mins	2 hr 35 mins

Nutritional Information:

Calories	395 kcal
Carbohydrates	**14.9 g**
Cholesterol	125 mg
Fat	21 g
Fiber	**6.6 g**
Protein	**40.1 g**
Sodium	683 mg

* Percent Daily Values are based on a 2,000 calorie diet.

Buko I

(Coconut Chiller)

Ingredients

- 2 fresh young coconuts
- 1 cup water
- 1 tbsp white sugar, or to taste
- ice cubes

Directions

- Cut the top of a coconut and pour its juice into a bowl.
- Slice the coconut into two pieces and scrap out its inner flesh into the bowl containing the juice.
- Now mix sugar and some water, and pour it over ice in a glass.
- Serve.

Serving: 2

Timing Information:

Preparation	Cooking	Total Time
15 mins		15 mins

Nutritional Information:

Calories	1430 kcal
Carbohydrates	66.7 g
Cholesterol	0 mg
Fat	133 g
Fiber	35.7 g
Protein	13.2 g
Sodium	87 mg

* Percent Daily Values are based on a 2,000 calorie diet.

BIKO

(FILIPINO SWEET BAKED RICE)

Ingredients:

- 4 cups uncooked glutinous white rice
- 6 cups cold water
- 1 (14 ounce) can coconut milk, divided
- 1 1/3 cups white sugar
- 1 1/3 cups brown sugar
- 3 tbsps coconut preserves (such as Phil Supreme)

Directions:

- Preheat your oven to 325 degrees F and grease the baking pan.
- Cook rice that has been soaked in water for at least 8 hours along with half a cup of coconut milk, white sugar and water until the rice is tender.
- Now pour this mixture into the already prepared baking pan and pour a boiled mixture of coconut milk, brown sugar and coconut preserves over the rice.
- Bake in the preheated oven for about 25 minutes and cut into squares.
- Serve.

•

Serving: 6

Timing Information:

Preparation	Cooking	Total Time
15 mins	45 mins	11 hr

Nutritional Information:

Calories	463 kcal
Carbohydrates	90.3 g
Cholesterol	0 mg
Fat	9.5 g
Fiber	2.1 g
Protein	5.4 g
Sodium	17 mg

* Percent Daily Values are based on a 2,000 calorie diet.

TULYA

Ingredients:

- 2 tbsps olive oil
- 1 onion, chopped
- 2 cloves garlic, minced
- 1 (2 inch) piece fresh ginger, peeled and grated
- 2 tbsps oyster sauce
- 1/2 cup water
- 2 1/4 pounds clams in shell, scrubbed

Directions:

- Cook onion, garlic and ginger in hot oil for about 5 minutes before adding oyster sauce and cooking for another 2 minutes.
- Pour water into the mix and cook for another two minutes while covering the pan.
- Now add clams and cook for another 5 minutes or until the clams have opened up.
- Discard all the unopened clams and serve.

Serving: 6

Timing Information:

Preparation	Cooking	Total Time
15 mins	10 mins	25 mins

Nutritional Information:

Calories	120 kcal
Carbohydrates	5.3 g
Cholesterol	20 mg
Fat	7.4 g
Fiber	0.6 g
Protein	8.1 g
Sodium	91 mg

* Percent Daily Values are based on a 2,000 calorie diet.

SATI BABI

Ingredients:

- 3 pounds pork butt roast, cut into 1 1/2 inch cubes
- 3/4 tsp salt
- 1/8 tsp ground black pepper
- 1 tbsp ground coriander
- 1 tbsp cumin seed
- 1/2 tsp vegetable oil
- 1/2 cup sliced onions
- 1 tbsp brown sugar
- 1/3 cup soy sauce
- 1/4 tsp ground ginger
- 3 limes, cut into wedges

Directions:

- At first you need to set a grill or grilling plate to medium heat and put some oil before starting anything else.
- Combine salt, pepper, coriander, cumin seed, and vegetable oil in a dish before adding pork and letting it stand for at least 20 minutes.
- Now add onion, ginger and soy sauce and place everything in the refrigerator for at least one hour after mixing it well.
- Thread these pork cubes onto the skewers
- Cook contents on the preheated grill or grilling plate for about 15 minutes or until tender.
- Sprinkle some lime juice before serving.
- Enjoy.

Serving: 6

Timing Information:

Preparation	Cooking	Total Time
15 mins	15 mins	1 hr 30 mins

Nutritional Information:

Calories	224 kcal
Carbohydrates	**6.6 g**
Cholesterol	71 mg
Fat	13 g
Fiber	**1.4 g**
Protein	**20.2 g**
Sodium	873 mg

* Percent Daily Values are based on a 2,000 calorie diet.

BARBECUED SPARERIBS

Ingredients:

- 1 (4 pound) package pork spareribs, rinsed and patted dry
- salt and ground black pepper to taste
- 1 cup water
- 1 cup sweet chili sauce

Directions:

- Preheat your oven to 350 degrees F and grease the baking pan.
- Add some salt and pepper over spareribs before putting them into the baking dish containing water.
- Cover with aluminum foil.
- Bake in the preheated oven for about 30 minutes before pouring chili sauce half of what we have and return it to the oven.
- Brush with chili sauce every five minutes and continue baking for 30 more minutes or until tender.
- Serve.

Serving: 6

Timing Information:

Preparation	Cooking	Total Time
10 mins	1 hr	1 hr 10 mins

Nutritional Information:

Calories	710 kcal
Carbohydrates	**20.6 g**
Cholesterol	192 mg
Fat	**48.4 g**
Fiber	**1.4 g**
Protein	**46.1 g**
Sodium	765 mg

* Percent Daily Values are based on a 2,000 calorie diet.

FILIPINO MELON DESSERT I

Ingredients

- 1 large ripe cantaloupe
- 2 quarts cold water
- 1 large honeydew melon

Directions

- Blend cantaloupe and place it in a pitcher.
- Now pour into it some water and refrigerate it for 12 hours or preferably overnight.
- Make small balls out of the honeydew melon using a spoon and add these balls before serving.

Serving: 6

Timing Information:

Preparation	Cooking	Total Time
20 mins		1 day

Nutritional Information:

Calories	123 kcal
Carbohydrates	30.5 g
Cholesterol	0 mg
Fat	0.6 g
Fiber	2.8 g
Protein	2.3 g
Sodium	70 mg

* Percent Daily Values are based on a 2,000 calorie diet.

CHICKEN ADOBO

Ingredients:

- 1 1/2 cups water
- 1 cup distilled white vinegar
- 4 tbsps soy sauce
- 1 tsp whole peppercorns
- 4 cloves garlic, crushed
- 2 tbsps salt
- 1 (2 to 3 pound) whole chicken, cut into pieces
- 2 tbsps vegetable oil

Directions:

- Mix water, salt, vinegar, peppercorns, garlic and soy sauce before adding chicken and cooking it over low heat for about 30 minutes or until the chicken is tender.
- Cook this chicken in hot oil until brown after removing it from the pot.
- Now put this chicken back into the pot and cook over medium heat until you see that the liquid has become thick.
- Serve.

Serving: 6

Timing Information:

Preparation	Cooking	Total Time
1 hr	15 mins	1 hr 15 mins

Nutritional Information:

Calories	340 kcal
Carbohydrates	2 g
Cholesterol	100 mg
Fat	**21.5 g**
Fiber	**0.2 g**
Protein	**32.5 g**
Sodium	3598 mg

* Percent Daily Values are based on a 2,000 calorie diet.

Empanada Pork Filling

Ingredients:

- 1 pound ground pork
- salt and pepper to taste
- 2 tbsps olive oil
- 1 onion, chopped
- 2 cloves garlic, minced
- 1 (9 ounce) box frozen peas and carrots
- 1 (1.5 ounce) box raisins
- 1 small potato, diced

Directions:

- Take out ground pork and cook it over medium heat in nonstick skillet for about 5 minutes or until you see that it is brown.
- Now cook onion and garlic in hot oil for about 5 minutes before adding browned pork into it and cooking it for another 5 minutes.
- Now add potato, raisins, peas and carrots into the skillet, and cook them for about 10 minutes or until the vegetables are tender.
- Allow this to cool down before filling into empanada dough.
- Serve.

Serving: 6

Timing Information:

Preparation	Cooking	Total Time
10 mins	15 mins	1 hr 25 mins

Nutritional Information:

Calories	67 kcal
Carbohydrates	4.4 g
Cholesterol	12 mg
Fat	3.9 g
Fiber	0.7 g
Protein	4 g
Sodium	19 mg

* Percent Daily Values are based on a 2,000 calorie diet.

Fried Tulingan (Mackerel)

Ingredients:

- 1 (3 1/2) pound whole mackerel, gutted and cleaned
- 2 cups water
- 1 tbsp tamarind soup base
- 1 tsp fish sauce
- oil for frying

Directions:

- Mix mackerel water, fish sauce and a tamarind soup base in a skillet, and cook over medium heat for about 15 minutes.
- Flip the fish once very carefully and cook for another 15 minutes before turning off the heat and letting it stand as it is for about one hour.
- Take out the fish and dry it with paper towels before deep frying it in large skillet for about 10 minutes.
- Serve.

Serving: 4

Timing Information:

Preparation	Cooking	Total Time
10 mins	40 mins	1 hr 50 mins

Nutritional Information:

Calories	974 kcal
Carbohydrates	**0.8 g**
Cholesterol	222 mg
Fat	70 g
Fiber	0 g
Protein	**77.6 g**
Sodium	841 mg

* Percent Daily Values are based on a 2,000 calorie diet.

SALMON STEW (ABALOS STYLE)

Ingredients:

- 1 tbsp olive oil
- 4 cloves garlic, minced
- 1 onion, diced
- 1 tomato, diced
- 1 (14.75 ounce) can pink salmon
- 2 1/2 cups water
- bay leaf (optional)
- salt and ground black pepper to taste
- 1 tsp fish sauce (optional)

Directions:

- Cook onion and garlic in hot oil for about 5 minutes before adding tomato and salmon into it.
- Cook for another 3 minutes and then add water, fish sauce, bay leaf, salt and pepper.
- Cover the skillet and cook for 20 minutes.
- Serve.

Serving: 4

Timing Information:

Preparation	Cooking	Total Time
10 mins	15 mins	25 mins

Nutritional Information:

Calories	223 kcal
Carbohydrates	4.8 g
Cholesterol	45 mg
Fat	11 g
Fiber	0.9 g
Protein	24.9 g
Sodium	466 mg

* Percent Daily Values are based on a 2,000 calorie diet.

FILIPINO FRUIT SALAD

Ingredients

- 1 (30 ounce) can fruit cocktail, drained
- 1 (15 ounce) can lychees, drained
- 1 (12 ounce) jar macapuno (coconut preserves), drained
- 1 (20 ounce) can palm seeds, drained
- 1 (15 ounce) can creamed corn
- 1 Red Delicious apple, cored and diced
- 1 Asian pear, cored and cubed
- 1 (8 ounce) container sour cream
- 1 (14 ounce) can sweetened condensed milk

Directions

- Combine all the ingredients mentioned above in a bowl and serve it cold.

Serving: 10

Timing Information:

Preparation	Cooking	Total Time
10 mins		1 hr 10 mins

Nutritional Information:

Calories	482 kcal
Carbohydrates	61.8 g
Cholesterol	23 mg
Fat	25.9 g
Fiber	2.9 g
Protein	9.8 g
Sodium	204 mg

* Percent Daily Values are based on a 2,000 calorie diet.

FILIPINO SPAGHETTI

Ingredients:

- 2 pounds spaghetti
- 1 tbsp vegetable oil
- 1 head garlic, minced
- 1 onion, chopped
- 1 pound ground beef
- 1 pound ground pork
- salt and pepper to taste
- 1 (26.5 ounce) can spaghetti sauce
- 1 (14 ounce) jar banana ketchup
- 1/4 cup white sugar
- 1/2 cup water
- 1 pound hot dogs, sliced diagonally
- 1/2 cup shredded Cheddar cheese

Directions:

- Cook spaghetti in boiling hot salty water over high heat for about 12 minutes or until the pasta is heated through.
- Drain it well using colander.
- Now cook onion and garlic in hot oil over medium heat for about 5 minutes before adding beef and pork, while seasoning it with some salt and pepper.
- Cook it until you see the brown color on the meat and then add spaghetti sauce, water, banana ketchup and sugar into it.
- Cook until you see that the sauce has thickened before adding hot dog slices and cooking it until the hot dogs are heated through.
- Pour this over spaghetti and also some cheddar cheese.
- Enjoy.

Serving: 6

Timing Information:

Preparation	Cooking	Total Time
10 mins	10 mins	20 mins

Nutritional Information:

Calories	708 kcal
Carbohydrates	82.9 g
Cholesterol	77 mg
Fat	27.4 g
Fiber	4.3 g
Protein	29.2 g
Sodium	1085 mg

* Percent Daily Values are based on a 2,000 calorie diet.

AVOCADO MILKSHAKES IN THE PHILIPPINES

Ingredients

- 1 avocado - peeled, pitted, and cubed
- 5 cubes ice
- 3 tbsps white sugar
- 1 1/3 cups milk
- 1 tsp fresh lemon or lime juice
- 1 scoop vanilla ice cream

Directions

- Blend all the ingredients mentioned above in a blender until required smoothness is achieved.
- Serve.

Serving: 6

Timing Information:

Preparation	Cooking	Total Time
5 mins		5 mins

Nutritional Information:

Calories	336 kcal
Carbohydrates	37.6 g
Cholesterol	18 mg
Fat	19.1 g
Fiber	6.8 g
Protein	7.8 g
Sodium	84 mg

* Percent Daily Values are based on a 2,000 calorie diet.

SINGKAMAS

(JICAMA SALAD)

Ingredients

- 1 large jicama, peeled and cut into matchsticks
- 1 red bell pepper, cut into long thin strips
- 1 green bell pepper, cut into long thin strips
- 1 small red onion, sliced into thin lengthwise slivers
- 2 green chile peppers, halved lengthwise, seeded, and cut into strips
- 1 (2 inch) piece fresh ginger root, thinly sliced
- 1 carrot, cut into matchsticks
- 1 cup water
- 2/3 cup vinegar
- 2/3 cup white sugar
- 1 tsp salt

Directions

- Mix jicama, red bell pepper, red onion, green chili peppers, ginger, green bell pepper and carrot in large sized bowl.
- In another bowl, mix water, salt, vinegar and sugar.
- Pour this mixture over the vegetables and refrigerate it for about 1 hour at least before serving it.

Serving: 10

Timing Information:

Preparation	Cooking	Total Time
30 mins		1 hr 30 mins

Nutritional Information:

Calories	113 kcal
Carbohydrates	27.5 g
Cholesterol	0 mg
Fat	0.2 g
Fiber	6.8 g
Protein	1.4 g
Sodium	244 mg

* Percent Daily Values are based on a 2,000 calorie diet.

Picadillo Filipino

(Hamburger Abalos Soup)

Ingredients

- 1 tbsp cooking oil
- 1 onion, diced
- 4 cloves garlic, minced
- 1 large tomato, diced
- 1 pound ground beef
- 4 cups water
- 1 large potato, diced
- 2 tbsps beef bouillon
- 2 tbsps fish sauce
- salt and pepper to taste

Directions

- Cook onions and garlic in hot oil over medium heat until tender add tomatoes and cook for another 3 minutes.
- Now add ground beef and cook for about 5 more minutes or until the color has turned brown.
- Add potato, fish sauce, pepper, beef bouillon, water and some salt into the pan and cook at low heat for 30 minutes while stirring regularly.
- Serve.

Serving: 6

Timing Information:

Preparation	Cooking	Total Time
20 mins	45 mins	1 hr 5 mins

Nutritional Information:

Calories	233 kcal
Carbohydrates	16.9 g
Cholesterol	46 mg
Fat	11.5 g
Fiber	2.4 g
Protein	15.4 g
Sodium	862 mg

* Percent Daily Values are based on a 2,000 calorie diet.

FISH SINIGANG

(TILAPIA)

Ingredients

- 1/2 pound tilapia fillets, cut into chunks
- 1 small head bok choy, chopped
- 2 medium tomatoes, cut into chunks
- 1 cup thinly sliced daikon radish
- 1/4 cup tamarind paste
- 3 cups water
- 2 dried red chile peppers(optional)

Directions

- Combine tilapia, radish, tomatoes, mixture of tamarind paste and water, chili peppers and bok choy.
- Bring the mixture to boil and cook for 5 minutes to get fish tender.
- Serve in appropriate bowls.

Serving: 10

Timing Information:

Preparation	Cooking	Total Time
5 mins	10 mins	15 mins

Nutritional Information:

Calories	112 kcal
Carbohydrates	13.4 g
Cholesterol	21 mg
Fat	1 g
Fiber	2.1 g
Protein	13.1 g
Sodium	63 mg

* Percent Daily Values are based on a 2,000 calorie diet.

Paksiw na Pata

(Pig's Feet Stew)

Ingredients

- 3 1/4 pounds pig's feet, rinsed and patted dry
- 1 1/2 cups vinegar
- 1 1/2 cups water
- 1/3 cup soy sauce
- 1 onion, diced
- 2 cloves garlic, crushed
- 1 tbsp whole black peppercorns, crushed
- 3 bay leaves
- 1 tbsp white sugar
- salt to taste

Directions

- Mix all the ingredients mentioned above in a pan and bring this mixture to boil for 3 minutes before turning the heat lower to medium and cooking for one full hour.
- Serve.

Serving: 5

Timing Information:

Preparation	Cooking	Total Time
10 mins	1hr 10 mins	1 hr 20 mins

Nutritional Information:

Calories	342 kcal
Carbohydrates	9.2 g
Cholesterol	138 mg
Fat	20.8 g
Fiber	1.2 g
Protein	30 g
Sodium	1061 mg

* Percent Daily Values are based on a 2,000 calorie diet.

Sinigang Na Baka

(Beef Based Veggie Soup)

Ingredients

- 2 tbsps canola oil
- 1 large onion, chopped
- 2 cloves garlic, chopped
- 1 pound beef stew meat, cut into 1 inch cubes
- 1 quart water
- 2 large tomatoes, diced
- 1/2 pound fresh green beans, rinsed and trimmed
- 1/2 medium head bok choy, cut into 1 1/2 inch strips
- 1 head fresh broccoli, cut into bite size pieces
- 1 (1.41 ounce) package tamarind soup base

Directions

- Cook onion and garlic in hot oil and then add beef to get it brown.
- Now add some water and bring it to a boil.
- Turn the heat down to medium and cook for 30 minutes.
- Cook for another 10 minutes after adding tomatoes and green beans.
- Now add tamarind soup mix, bok choy and some broccoli into the mix and cook for 10 more minutes to get everything tender.

Serving: 6
Timing Information:

Preparation	Cooking	Total Time
15 mins	45 mins	1 hr

Nutritional Information:

Calories	304 kcal
Carbohydrates	15 g
Cholesterol	51 mg
Fat	19.7 g
Fiber	4.5 g
Protein	17.8 g
Sodium	1405 mg

* Percent Daily Values are based on a 2,000 calorie diet.

MELON CHILLER

Ingredients

- 1 cantaloupe, halved and seeded
- 1 gallon water
- 2 cups white sugar
- ice cubes, as needed

Directions

- Take out the meat of cantaloupe and place into a punch bowl with a melon baller add sugar and some water after placing this into bowl.
- Mix it well and serve it cold.

Serving: 6

Timing Information:

Preparation	Cooking	Total Time
20 mins		1 hr 5 mins

Nutritional Information:

Calories	174 kcal
Carbohydrates	44.5 g
Cholesterol	0 mg
Fat	0.1 g
Fiber	0.5 g
Protein	0.5 g
Sodium	23 mg

* Percent Daily Values are based on a 2,000 calorie diet.

Filipino Chicken Stew

Ingredients

- 2 tbsps sesame oil
- 2 pounds boneless chicken pieces, cut into strips
- 2 tbsps fresh lemon juice
- 2 tbsps soy sauce
- 2 (15 ounce) cans coconut milk
- 1/4 cup red curry paste
- 1/4 cup flour
- 2 red bell peppers, chopped
- 1 sweet onion, chopped
- 1 red onion, chopped
- 2 cloves garlic, minced
- 2 large potatoes, cubed
- 2 (8 ounce) cans sliced bamboo shoots, drained
- 2 (8 ounce) cans sliced water chestnuts, drained
- 2 (8 ounce) cans baby corn, drained
- 1 (12 ounce) can sliced mushrooms, drained
- 1/4 cup chopped cilantro

Directions

- Cook chicken, lemon juice, and soy sauce in hot sesame oil over medium heat for 5 minutes and in a bowl mix flour, coconut milk and curry paste, and add this mixture to the pan.
- Now put bell pepper, red onion, garlic, potatoes, bamboo shoots, water chestnuts, sweet onion and mushrooms into the pan and cook at low heat for 45 minutes before adding cilantro and removing it from heat.
- Serve

Serving: 8

Timing Information:

Preparation	Cooking	Total Time
25 mins	50 mins	1 hr 15 mins

Nutritional Information:

Calories	554 kcal
Carbohydrates	28.4 g
Cholesterol	57 mg
Fat	32.3 g
Fiber	11.7 g
Protein	28.4 g
Sodium	645 mg

* Percent Daily Values are based on a 2,000 calorie diet.

CHAMPORADO

Ingredients

- 1 cup glutinous sweet rice
- 2 cups light coconut milk
- 1/2 cup cocoa powder
- 1 cup white sugar
- 1 tsp salt
- 1 cup thick coconut milk

Directions

- Bring the mixture of sweet rice and coconut milk to boil for 10 minutes while stirring regularly.
- Now add sugar, salt and cocoa power into this rice and cook at low heat for about 10 minutes or until you see that the rice is tender.
- Pour thick coconut milk into it and serve.

Serving: 8

Timing Information:

Preparation	Cooking	Total Time
5 mins	30 mins	35 mins

Nutritional Information:

Calories	428 kcal
Carbohydrates	53.4 g
Cholesterol	0 mg
Fat	25.2 g
Fiber	4.3 g
Protein	4.9 g
Sodium	407 mg

* Percent Daily Values are based on a 2,000 calorie diet.

Maja Blanca Maiz

(Corn Pudding)

Ingredients

- 1 2/3 cups coconut milk
- 1 (14.5 ounce) can cream-style corn
- 1 cup rice flour
- 1 cup white sugar

Directions

- Mix all the ingredients mentioned above thoroughly in a pan over medium heat and cook for 30 minutes or until the required thickness is achieved.
- Now pour everything into a serving platter and let it cool.
- Serve.

Serving: 10

Timing Information:

Preparation	Cooking	Total Time
5 mins	30 mins	1 hr 35 mins

Nutritional Information:

Calories	239 kcal
Carbohydrates	41.1 g
Cholesterol	0 mg
Fat	8.4 g
Fiber	1.3 g
Protein	2.4 g
Sodium	121 mg

* Percent Daily Values are based on a 2,000 calorie diet.

Cassava Cake

Ingredients

- 2 cups grated, peeled yucca
- 2 eggs, beaten
- 1 (12 ounce) can evaporated milk
- 1 (14 ounce) can sweetened condensed milk
- 1 (14 ounce) can coconut milk

Directions

- Set your oven to 350 degrees F before continuing.
- Mix all the ingredients mentioned above in a bowl and pour this mixture into a baking dish.
- Bake this for one hour before switching on the broiler and letting it turn the top of the cake brown.
- Refrigerate before serving.

Serving: 1

Timing Information:

Preparation	Cooking	Total Time
20 mins	1 hr	2 hr 20 mins

Nutritional Information:

Calories	329 kcal
Carbohydrates	41.6 g
Cholesterol	60 mg
Fat	15.5 g
Fiber	1.2 g
Protein	8 g
Sodium	111 mg

* Percent Daily Values are based on a 2,000 calorie diet.

BUTTER COOKIES IN THE PHILIPPINES

Ingredients

- 1 cup butter, softened
- 1 cup white sugar
- 3 eggs
- 3 2/3 cups cornstarch
- 1 tsp cream of tartar
- 1 tsp baking powder

Directions

- Set your oven at 350 degrees F and grease the cookie sheets before continuing.
- Mix butter and sugar, and then add eggs one by one.
- Now add cornstarch, cream of tartar and some baking powder.
- Mix them well and place 1 inch balls over the greased cookie sheets.
- Bake this for 12 minutes in the preheated oven and then let it cool down before serving.

Serving: 5 dozen

Timing Information:

Preparation	Cooking	Total Time
5 mins	12 mins	17 mins

Nutritional Information:

Calories	74 kcal
Carbohydrates	10.5 g
Cholesterol	17 mg
Fat	3.3 g
Fiber	0.1 g
Protein	0.4 g
Sodium	34 mg

* Percent Daily Values are based on a 2,000 calorie diet.

FILIPINO MELON DESSERT II

Ingredients

- 4 pounds cantaloupe, shredded
- 1 (12 fluid ounce) can of evaporated milk
- 2 quarts water
- 1 1/4 cups white sugar

Directions

- Mix all the ingredients mentioned above thoroughly and then refrigerate for some time.
- Divide this into molds and freeze this for about 6 hours or until it is firm enough.

Serving: 20

Timing Information:

Preparation	Cooking	Total Time
15 mins		6 hr 15 mins

Nutritional Information:

Calories	105 kcal
Carbohydrates	21.8 g
Cholesterol	5 mg
Fat	1.6 g
Fiber	0.8 g
Protein	2 g
Sodium	37 mg

* Percent Daily Values are based on a 2,000 calorie diet.

CHOCOLATE-ORANGE RICE PUDDING

Ingredients

- 5 1/2 cups milk
- 1 cup Arborio rice
- 2/3 cup white sugar
- 2 tbsps orange juice
- 1 1/2 tsps grated orange zest
- 2 tbsps orange liqueur
- 1 tbsp unsweetened cocoa powder
- 1 cup semisweet chocolate chips

Directions

- Mix rice, orange zest, milk and orange juice in a pan and bring it to a boil before turning down the heat to medium and cooking for another 40 minutes or until the rice is tender.
- Add orange liqueur and cocoa powder into the rice mixture after removing it from the heat.
- Also add some chocolate chips and let it melt.
- Serve.

Serving: 8

Timing Information:

Preparation	Cooking	Total Time
10 mins	40 mins	50 mins

Nutritional Information:

Calories	356 kcal
Carbohydrates	60.6 g
Cholesterol	13 mg
Fat	9.7 g
Fiber	1.8 g
Protein	8.3 g
Sodium	72 mg

* Percent Daily Values are based on a 2,000 calorie diet.

GARLIC RICE

Ingredients

- 2 tbsps vegetable oil
- 1 1/2 tbsps chopped garlic
- 2 tbsps ground pork
- 4 cups cooked white rice
- 1 1/2 tsps garlic salt
- ground black pepper to taste

Directions

- Cook garlic and ground pork in hot oil over medium heat until golden brown.
- Now add cooked white rice and add some garlic and pepper according to your taste.
- Cook for about 3 minutes to get it mixed thoroughly.
- Serve.

Serving: 8

Timing Information:

Preparation	Cooking	Total Time
5 mins	5 mins	10 mins

Nutritional Information:

Calories	293 kcal
Carbohydrates	45.9 g
Cholesterol	6 mg
Fat	9 g
Fiber	0.8 g
Protein	5.9 g
Sodium	686 mg

* Percent Daily Values are based on a 2,000 calorie diet.

Corned Beef Hash In the Philippines

Ingredients

- 1 tbsp vegetable oil
- 4 cloves garlic, chopped
- 1 onion, diced
- 1 tomato, chopped
- 1 large potato, diced
- 1 (12 ounce) can corned beef
- salt and pepper to taste

Directions

- Cook onion and garlic over in hot oil over medium heat and then add tomatoes and potatoes.
- Cook for 10 minutes and then add beef, and cook for another 10 minutes.
- Add some salt and pepper before serving.
- Enjoy.

Serving: 4

Timing Information:

Preparation	Cooking	Total Time
15 mins	30 mins	45 mins

Nutritional Information:

Calories	333 kcal
Carbohydrates	21.1 g
Cholesterol	72 mg
Fat	16.2 g
Fiber	2.8 g
Protein	25.5 g
Sodium	853 mg

* Percent Daily Values are based on a 2,000 calorie diet.

Corned Beef Waffles

Ingredients

- 2 eggs
- 1 1/4 cups milk
- 2 tsps cooking oil
- 1 1/2 cups all-purpose flour
- 1 pinch salt
- 2 tsps baking powder
- 1/2 (12 ounce) can corned beef, broken into pieces

Directions

- Heat a waffle iron before continuing.
- Combine milk, oil and eggs in a bowl and in a separate bowl mix flour salt and baking powder.
- Combine both mixtures and add beef.
- Put this mixture into the preheated waffle iron and cook it until the waffles are golden in color.
- Serve it with butter.

Serving: 10

Timing Information:

Preparation	Cooking	Total Time
10 mins	10 mins	20 mins

Nutritional Information:

Calories	148 kcal
Carbohydrates	16 g
Cholesterol	54 mg
Fat	5.2 g
Fiber	0.5 g
Protein	8.8 g
Sodium	268 mg

* Percent Daily Values are based on a 2,000 calorie diet.

Mango Bread

Ingredients

- 2 cups all-purpose flour
- 2 tsps ground cinnamon
- 2 tsps baking soda
- 1/2 tsp salt
- 1 1/4 cups white sugar
- 2 eggs
- 3/4 cup vegetable oil
- 2 1/2 cups mangos, peeled, seeded and chopped
- 1 tsp lemon juice
- 1/4 cup raisins

Directions

- Mix all the dry ingredients mentioned above and then add eggs beaten in oil to this mixture.
- Now add mangoes, raisins and lemon.
- Pour this into two different pans and bake at 350 degrees F for 60 minutes.
- Serve.

Serving: 2

Timing Information:

Preparation	Cooking	Total Time
20 mins	1 hr	1 hr 20 mins

Nutritional Information:

Calories	193 kcal
Carbohydrates	27.2 g
Cholesterol	19 mg
Fat	8.9 g
Fiber	0.9 g
Protein	2.1 g
Sodium	192 mg

* Percent Daily Values are based on a 2,000 calorie diet.

Barbecued Pork Kebabs

Ingredients

- 1 cup white sugar
- 1 cup soy sauce
- 1 onion, diced
- 5 cloves garlic, chopped
- 1 tsp ground black pepper
- 1 (4 pound) boneless pork loin, cut into 1 1/2-inch cubes
- 10 bamboo skewers, soaked in water for 30 minutes

Directions

- Mix sugar, black pepper, soy sauce, garlic and onion in an appropriate bowl.
- Refrigerate for about 2 hours after adding pork.
- Preheat the grill or grilling plate to a high heat and put some oil before progressing.
- Now cook skewers with pork on the preheated grill for about 5 minutes each side.
- Serve.

NOTE: If using a grilling plate increase the amount of cooking time until you find your meat completely cooked.

Serving: 10

Timing Information:

Preparation	Cooking	Total Time
15 mins	15 mins	2 hr 30 mins

Nutritional Information:

Calories	369 kcal
Carbohydrates	24.7 g
Cholesterol	88 mg
Fat	15.8 g
Fiber	0.7 g
Protein	31.1 g
Sodium	1508 mg

* Percent Daily Values are based on a 2,000 calorie diet.

GUINATAAN HITO

(CATFISH)

Ingredients

- 2 tbsps cooking oil
- 1 onion, chopped
- 2 cloves garlic, crushed
- 4 (4 ounce) catfish fillets
- salt and pepper to taste
- 1 1/2 cups coconut milk

Directions

- Cook onion and garlic in hot oil for about 10 minutes and then add catfish, and cook for another 2 minutes.
- Now add coconut milk and cook for another 10 minutes or until the coconut milk gets oily.
- Serve with rice.

Serving: 4

Timing Information:

Preparation	Cooking	Total Time
10 mins	30 mins	40 mins

Nutritional Information:

Calories	388 kcal
Carbohydrates	5.4 g
Cholesterol	51 mg
Fat	33.2 g
Fiber	1.4 g
Protein	19.1 g
Sodium	64 mg

* Percent Daily Values are based on a 2,000 calorie diet.

FILIPINO PORK ADOBO

Ingredients

- 1 cup distilled white vinegar
- 1 cup soy sauce
- 1/2 cup ketchup
- 1 tbsp minced garlic
- 3 bay leaves
- 1 tsp fresh-ground black pepper
- 2 1/2 pounds lean pork, cut into 1 inch cubes
- 1 pound small green beans, trimmed (optional)

Directions

- Combine pork, bay leaves, vinegar, garlic, soy sauce and ketchup, and bring them to boil at high heat.
- Now turn down the heat to low and cook for another two and a half hours.
- If you are using green beans in this recipe then add them in the last hour to get them tender.
- Serve.

Serving: 6

Timing Information:

Preparation	Cooking	Total Time
20 mins	2 hr 30 mins	2 hr 50 mins

Nutritional Information:

Calories	337 kcal
Carbohydrates	**14.4 g**
Cholesterol	90 mg
Fat	**15.5 g**
Fiber	**3.1 g**
Protein	**35.1 g**
Sodium	2687 mg

* Percent Daily Values are based on a 2,000 calorie diet.

Buko II

(Filipino Coconut Pie Dessert)

Ingredients

- 1 fresh young coconut, drained with meat removed and chopped
- 2 (12 fluid ounce) cans of evaporated milk
- 1 (14 ounce) can sweetened condensed milk
- 4 eggs, beaten
- 1/4 cup white sugar
- 1 pinch salt

Directions

- Set your oven to 350 degrees F before continuing.
- Now combine all the ingredients mentioned above in a large bowl and pour into a baking dish.
- Fill the baking with enough water to cover half.
- Now bake everything in the preheated oven for about 60 minutes.
- Cool it down and serve.

Serving: 6

Timing Information:

Preparation	Cooking	Total Time
20 mins	1 hr	1 hr 50 mins

Nutritional Information:

Calories	693 kcal
Carbohydrates	66.9 g
Cholesterol	183 mg
Fat	40.7 g
Fiber	6 g
Protein	20.1 g
Sodium	276 mg

* Percent Daily Values are based on a 2,000 calorie diet.

CHAPTER 3: THAI RECIPES
EASY THAI COOKBOOK

Classical Pad Thai Noodles I

Ingredients

- 2/3 cup dried rice vermicelli
- 1/4 cup peanut oil
- 2/3 cup thinly sliced firm tofu
- 1 large egg, beaten
- 4 cloves garlic, finely chopped
- 1/4 cup vegetable broth
- 2 tbsps fresh lime juice
- 2 tbsps soy sauce
- 1 tbsp white sugar
- 1 tsp salt
- 1/2 tsp dried red chili flakes
- 3 tbsps chopped peanuts
- 1 pound bean sprouts, divided
- 3 green onions, whites cut thinly across and greens sliced into thin lengths - divided
- 3 tbsps chopped peanuts
- 2 limes, cut into wedges for garnish

Directions

- Put rice vermicelli noodles in hot water for about 30 minutes before draining the water.
- Cook tofu in hot oil until golden brown before draining it with paper tower.
- Reserve 1 tbsp of oil for later use and cook egg in the remaining hot oil until done, and set them aside for later use.
- Now cook noodles and garlic in the hot reserved oil, while coating them well with this oil along the way.
- In this pan containing noodles; add tofu, salt, chili flakes, egg and 3 tbsps peanuts, and mix all this very thoroughly.

- Also add bean sprouts and green onion into it, while reserving some for the garnishing purposes.
- Cook all this for two minutes before transferring to a serving platter.
- Garnish this with peanuts and the reserved vegetables before placing some lime wedges around the platter to make this dish more attractive.
- Serve.

Serving: 4

Timing Information:

Preparation	Cooking	Total Time
30 mins	20 mins	2 hrs

Nutritional Information:

Calories	397 kcal
Carbohydrates	39.5 g
Cholesterol	41 mg
Fat	23.3 g
Fiber	5 g
Protein	13.2 g
Sodium	1234 mg

* Percent Daily Values are based on a 2,000 calorie diet.

A PESTO FROM THAILAND

Ingredients

- 1 bunch cilantro
- 1/4 cup peanut butter
- 3 cloves garlic, minced
- 3 tbsps extra-virgin olive oil
- 2 tbsps minced fresh ginger
- 1 1/2 tbsps fish sauce
- 1 tbsp brown sugar
- 1/2 tsp cayenne pepper

Directions

- Put all the ingredients that are mentioned above in a blender and blend it until you see that the required smoothness is achieved.

Serving: 12

Timing Information:

Preparation	Cooking	Total Time
10 mins		10 mins

Nutritional Information:

Calories	84 kcal
Carbohydrates	3.4 g
Cholesterol	0 mg
Fat	7.4 g
Fiber	0.6 g
Protein	1.9 g
Sodium	197 mg

* Percent Daily Values are based on a 2,000 calorie diet.

Easy Hummus Thai Style

Ingredients

- 1/4 cup coconut oil
- 2 large cloves garlic, very thinly sliced
- 2 cups cooked garbanzo beans
- 1/4 cup fresh lime juice
- 1/4 cup peanut butter
- 1/4 cup coconut milk
- 1/4 cup sweet chili sauce
- 1/4 cup minced lemon grass
- 1/4 cup minced fresh Thai basil leaves
- 1 tbsp grated fresh ginger
- 2 tsps green curry paste
- 1 jalapeno pepper, minced
- 1/2 tsp salt
- 1 pinch cayenne pepper(optional)
- 1 pinch chili powder (optional)

Directions

- Cook garlic in hot coconut oil for about one minute and transfer it to a bowl.
- Put cooled garlic mixture, lime juice, coconut milk, chili sauce, lemon grass, basil, ginger, curry paste, garbanzo beans, jalapeno pepper, salt, peanut butter, cayenne pepper and chili in a blender and blend it until you find that it is smooth.
- Serve.

Serving: 12

Timing Information:

Preparation	Cooking	Total Time
15 mins	5 mins	30 mins

Nutritional Information:

Calories	142 kcal
Carbohydrates	13.8 g
Cholesterol	0 mg
Fat	9.4 g
Fiber	2.4 g
Protein	3.9 g
Sodium	315 mg

* Percent Daily Values are based on a 2,000 calorie diet.

Classical Pad Thai Noodles II

Ingredients

- 1 (6.75 ounce) package thin rice noodles
- 2 tbsps vegetable oil
- 3 ounces fried tofu, sliced into thin strips
- 1 clove garlic, minced
- 1 egg
- 1 tbsp soy sauce
- 1 pinch white sugar
- 2 tbsps chopped peanuts
- 1 cup fresh bean sprouts
- 1 tbsp chopped fresh cilantro
- 1 lime, cut into wedges

Directions

- In a heatproof bowl containing noodles, pour boiling water and let it stand as it is for about five minutes before draining the water and setting it aside for later use.
- Fry garlic in hot oil until brown before adding noodles frying it for about one minute.
- Now add egg into it and break it up when it starts to get solid, and mix it well into the noodles.
- Now add soy sauce, tofu, cilantro, bean sprouts, sugar and peanuts into it and mix it well.
- Remove from heat and add lime wedges just before you serve.

Serving: 4

Timing Information:

Preparation	Cooking	Total Time
15 mins	10 mins	25 mins

Nutritional Information:

Calories	352 kcal
Carbohydrates	46.8 g
Cholesterol	46 mg
Fat	15 g
Fiber	3 g
Protein	9.2 g
Sodium	335 mg

* Percent Daily Values are based on a 2,000 calorie diet.

Super Easy Coconut Soup Thai-Style

Ingredients

- 1 pound medium shrimp - peeled and deveined
- 2 (13.5 ounce) cans canned coconut milk
- 2 cups water
- 1 (1 inch) piece galangal, thinly sliced
- 4 stalks lemon grass, bruised and chopped
- 10 kaffir lime leaves, torn in half
- 1 pound shiitake mushrooms, sliced
- 1/4 cup lime juice
- 3 tbsps fish sauce
- 1/4 cup brown sugar
- 1 tsp curry powder
- 1 tbsp green onion, thinly sliced
- 1 tsp dried red pepper flakes

Directions

- Cook shrimp in boiling water until tender.
- Put coconut milk, water, lime leaves, galangal and lemon grass in a large sized pan and heat it up for about 10 minutes before transferring the coconut milk into a new pan, while discarding all the spices.
- Heat up shiitake mushrooms in the coconut milk for five minutes before adding lime juice, curry powder, brown sugar and fish sauce into it.
- When you want to serve it, heat up the shrimp in this soup for some time before pouring this into serving bowls.

Serving: 8

Timing Information:

Preparation	Cooking	Total Time
15 mins	25 mins	40 mins

Nutritional Information:

Calories	314 kcal
Carbohydrates	17.2 g
Cholesterol	86 mg
Fat	21.6 g
Fiber	2.1 g
Protein	15.3 g
Sodium	523 mg

* Percent Daily Values are based on a 2,000 calorie diet.

Curry Thai Inspired Chicken with Pineapple

Ingredients

- 2 cups uncooked jasmine rice
- 1 quart water
- 1/4 cup red curry paste
- 2 (13.5 ounce) cans coconut milk
- 2 skinless, boneless chicken breast halves - cut into thin strips
- 3 tbsps fish sauce
- 1/4 cup white sugar
- 1 1/2 cups sliced bamboo shoots, drained
- 1/2 red bell pepper, julienned
- 1/2 green bell pepper, julienned
- 1/2 small onion, chopped
- 1 cup pineapple chunks, drained

Directions

- Bring the mixture of rice and water to boil before turning the heat down to low and cooking for 25 minutes.
- Add coconut milk, bamboo shoots, chicken, sugar and fish sauce to the mixture of curry paste and 1 can coconut milk in a pan before bringing all this to boil and cooking for 15 minutes.
- Into this mixture, add red bell pepper, onion and green bell pepper, and cook all this for ten more minutes or until you see that the peppers are tender.
- Add pineapple after removing from heat and serve this on top of cooked rice.

Serving: 6

Timing Information:

Preparation	Cooking	Total Time
15 mins	35 mins	50 mins

Nutritional Information:

Calories	623 kcal
Carbohydrates	77.5 g
Cholesterol	20 mg
Fat	34.5 g
Fiber	3.5 g
Protein	20.3 g
Sodium	781 mg

* Percent Daily Values are based on a 2,000 calorie diet.

Simple and Easy Classical Peanut Sauce

Ingredients

- 1/4 cup creamy peanut butter
- 3 cloves garlic, minced
- 1/4 cup brown sugar
- 1/4 cup mayonnaise
- 1/4 cup soy sauce
- 2 tbsps fresh lemon juice

Directions

- Whisk all the ingredients that are mentioned above in a medium sized bowl and refrigerate it for at least two hours before you serve it to anyone.

Serving: 6

Timing Information:

Preparation	Cooking	Total Time
10 mins		10 mins

Nutritional Information:

Calories	130 kcal
Carbohydrates	9.8 g
Cholesterol	3 mg
Fat	9.5 g
Fiber	0.6 g
Protein	2.7 g
Sodium	529 mg

* Percent Daily Values are based on a 2,000 calorie diet.

Vegetable Soup In Thailand

Ingredients

- 1 cup uncooked brown rice
- 2 cups water
- 3 tbsps olive oil
- 1 sweet onion, chopped
- 4 cloves garlic, minced
- 1/4 cup chopped fresh ginger root
- 1 cup chopped carrots
- 4 cups chopped broccoli
- 1 red bell pepper, diced
- 1 (14 ounce) can light coconut milk
- 6 cups vegetable broth
- 1 cup white wine
- 3 tbsps fish sauce
- 2 tbsps soy sauce
- 3 Thai chili peppers
- 2 tbsps chopped fresh lemon grass
- 1 tbsp Thai pepper garlic sauce
- 1 tsp saffron
- 3/4 cup plain yogurt
- fresh cilantro, for garnish

Directions

- Bring the mixture of rice and water to boil before turning the heat down to low and cooking for 45 minutes.
- Cook ginger, carrots, garlic and onion in hot olive oil for about five minutes before you add broccoli, coconut milk, broth, wine, soy sauce, Thai chili peppers, red bell pepper, lemon grass, fish sauce, garlic sauce, and saffron into it and cook for another 25 minutes.
- Now blend this soup in batches in a blender until you get the required smoothness.
- Mix yoghurt and cooked rice very thoroughly with this soup.
- Garnish with cilantro before you serve.

Serving: 12

Timing Information:

Preparation	Cooking	Total Time
15 mins	1 hr 15 mins	1 hr 30 mins

Nutritional Information:

Calories	183 kcal
Carbohydrates	**21.4 g**
Cholesterol	< 1 mg
Fat	**7.4 g**
Fiber	3 g
Protein	**4.4 g**
Sodium	749 mg

* Percent Daily Values are based on a 2,000 calorie diet.

THE BEST ORANGE THAI CHICKEN

Ingredients

- 2 tbsps olive oil
- 3 carrots, cut into matchsticks
- 1/2 tsp minced fresh ginger root
- 1 clove garlic, minced
- 2 tbsps olive oil
- 2 skinless, boneless chicken breast halves, cut into small pieces
- 1/2 cup water
- 1/2 cup peanuts
- 1/3 cup orange juice
- 1/3 cup soy sauce
- 1/3 cup brown sugar
- 2 tbsps ketchup
- 1 tsp crushed red pepper flakes
- 2 tbsps cornstarch

Directions

- Cook carrots, garlic and ginger in hot olive oil for about 5 minutes before transferring it to a bowl.
- Cook chicken in hot olive oil for about 10 minutes before adding carrot mixture, water, brown sugar , orange juice, soy sauce, peanuts, ketchup, and red pepper flakes into this, and cooking for another 5 minutes.
- Take out ¼ cup of sauce from the pan and add cornstarch into it.
- Add this cornstarch mixture back to the chicken and cook until you see that the required thickness has been reached.

Serving: 12

Timing Information:

Preparation	Cooking	Total Time
15 mins	25 mins	40 mins

Nutritional Information:

Calories	427 kcal
Carbohydrates	37.1 g
Cholesterol	32 mg
Fat	24.3 g
Fiber	3.5 g
Protein	18.4 g
Sodium	1360 mg

* Percent Daily Values are based on a 2,000 calorie diet.

Thai Broccoli Mix

Ingredients

- 2 tbsps olive oil
- 2 large skinless, boneless chicken breast halves, cut into bite-size pieces
- 1 (12 ounce) package broccoli coleslaw mix
- 1 tsp sesame oil, or to taste
- 1/2 cup water
- 1/2 cup peanut sauce (such as House of Tsang®), or to taste
- 1 pinch salt to taste

Directions

- Cook chicken in hot olive oil for about 5 minutes before you add water, broccoli and sesame oil.
- Cook this on medium heat for about 15 minutes or until you see that the broccoli slaw is tender.
- Do add some peanut sauce and salt according to your taste before serving.

Serving: 4

Timing Information:

Preparation	Cooking	Total Time
10 mins	20 mins	30 mins

Nutritional Information:

Calories	315 kcal
Carbohydrates	8.2 g
Cholesterol	65 mg
Fat	18.9 g
Fiber	3.2 g
Protein	28.3 g
Sodium	275 mg

* Percent Daily Values are based on a 2,000 calorie diet.

A Uniquely Simple Cumber Soup with Thai Roots

Ingredients

- 1 tbsp vegetable oil
- 3 cucumbers, peeled and diced
- 1/2 cup chopped green onion
- 2 1/2 cups chicken broth
- 1 1/2 tbsps lemon juice
- 1 tsp white sugar
- salt and ground black pepper to taste

Directions

- Cook cucumber in hot olive oil for about 5 minutes before adding green onions and cooking for another five minutes.
- Add chicken broth, sugar and lemon juice into it before bringing all this to boil.
- Turn down the heat to low and cook for another 20 minutes before adding salt and black pepper according to your taste.
- Serve.

Serving: 4

Timing Information:

Preparation	Cooking	Total Time
15 mins	30 mins	45 mins

Nutritional Information:

Calories	67 kcal
Carbohydrates	6.8 g
Cholesterol	3 mg
Fat	4 g
Fiber	1.4 g
Protein	1.7 g
Sodium	702 mg

* Percent Daily Values are based on a 2,000 calorie diet.

BBQ Chicken Thai Style

Ingredients

- 1 bunch fresh cilantro with roots
- 3 cloves garlic, peeled
- 3 small red hot chili peppers, seeded and chopped
- 1 tsp ground turmeric
- 1 tsp curry powder
- 1 tbsp white sugar
- 1 pinch salt
- 3 tbsps fish sauce
- 1 (3 pound) chicken, cut into pieces
- 1/4 cup coconut milk

Directions

- At first you need to set a grill or grilling plate to medium heat and put some oil before starting anything else.
- Put minced cilantro roots, salt, leaves, chili peppers, curry powder, turmeric, sugar, fish sauce, garlic in a blender and blend until you see that the required smoothness is achieved.
- Combine this paste and chicken in large bowl, and refrigerate it for at least three hours for margination.
- Cook this on the preheated grill for about 15 minutes each side or until tender, while brushing it regularly with coconut milk.
- Serve.

NOTE: Adjust grilling times accordingly if using a grilling plate instead of a conventional grill.

Serving: 4

Timing Information:

Preparation	Cooking	Total Time
15 mins	30 mins	4 hr 45 mins

Nutritional Information:

Calories	564 kcal
Carbohydrates	**52.4 g**
Cholesterol	230 mg
Fat	**19.3 g**
Fiber	**4.3 g**
Protein	**46.3 g**
Sodium	375 mg

* Percent Daily Values are based on a 2,000 calorie diet.

CHARONG'S FAVORITE THAI SOUP OF GINGER

Ingredients

- 3 cups coconut milk
- 2 cups water
- 1/2 pound skinless, boneless chicken breast halves - cut into thin strips
- 3 tbsps minced fresh ginger root
- 2 tbsps fish sauce, or to taste
- 1/4 cup fresh lime juice
- 2 tbsps sliced green onions
- 1 tbsp chopped fresh cilantro

Directions

- Bring the mixture of coconut milk and water to boil before adding chicken strips, and cooking it for three minutes on medium heat or until you see that the chicken is cooked through.
- Now add ginger, green onions, lime juice, cilantro and fish sauce into it.
- Mix it well and serve.

Serving: 4

Timing Information:

Preparation	Cooking	Total Time
15 mins	10 mins	25 mins

Nutritional Information:

Calories	415 kcal
Carbohydrates	7.3 g
Cholesterol	29 mg
Fat	39 g
Fiber	2.1 g
Protein	14.4 g
Sodium	598 mg

* Percent Daily Values are based on a 2,000 calorie diet.

CHICKEN CURRY I

Ingredients

- 1 tbsp olive oil
- 3 tbsps Thai yellow curry paste (such as Mae Ploy®)
- 1 pound cooked skinless, boneless chicken breast, cut into bite-size pieces
- 2 (14 ounce) cans coconut milk
- 1 cup chicken stock
- 1 yellow onion, chopped
- 3 small red potatoes, cut into cubes, or as needed
- 3 red Thai chili peppers, chopped with seeds, or more to taste
- 1 tsp fish sauce

Directions

- Mix curry paste in hot oil before adding chicken and coating it well.
- Add 1 can coconut milk and cook it for five minutes before adding the rest of the coconut milk, onion, potatoes, chicken stock and chili peppers into it and bringing all this to boil.
- Turn the heat down to low and cook for 25 minutes or until the potatoes are tender.
- Add fish sauce into before serving.
- Enjoy.

Serving: 6

Timing Information:

Preparation	Cooking	Total Time
15 mins	40 mins	55 mins

Nutritional Information:

Calories	500 kcal
Carbohydrates	22.1 g
Cholesterol	58 mg
Fat	36.1 g
Fiber	3.6 g
Protein	25.8 g
Sodium	437 mg

* Percent Daily Values are based on a 2,000 calorie diet.

Chicken Curry II

Ingredients

- 1 tbsp canola oil
- 2 tbsps green curry paste
- 1 pound boneless skinless chicken breasts, cut into bite-size pieces
- 1 small onion, thinly sliced
- 1 red pepper, cut into thin strips, then cut crosswise in half
- 1 green pepper, cut into thin strips, then cut crosswise in half
- 4 ounces cream cheese, cubed
- 1/4 cup milk
- 1/8 tsp white pepper
- 2 cups hot cooked long-grain white rice

Directions

- Combine curry paste and hot oil before adding chicken and onions.
- Cook this for about 8 minutes before adding green and red peppers, and cooking for another five minutes.
- Now add cream cheese, white pepper and milk, and cook until you see that the cheese has melted.
- Serve this on top of rice.
- Enjoy.

Serving: 4

Timing Information:

Preparation	Cooking	Total Time
15 mins		35 mins

Nutritional Information:

Calories	621 kcal
Carbohydrates	86.7 g
Cholesterol	91 mg
Fat	19.4 g
Fiber	2.1 g
Protein	35.2 g
Sodium	316 mg

* Percent Daily Values are based on a 2,000 calorie diet.

A Thai Soup of Veggies

Ingredients

- 1/4 cup butter
- 6 tomatoes, peeled and quartered
- 3 zucchini, cut into chunks
- 1 yellow onion, cut in half and quartered
- 1 red bell pepper, chopped
- 3 cloves garlic, roughly chopped
- 1/4 cup chopped fresh cilantro leaves
- 1 tbsp chopped fresh basil (preferably Thai basil)
- 1 tbsp lime juice
- 1 pinch salt
- 2 1/2 cups milk
- 3 tbsps coconut butter
- 1 tbsp curry powder
- 1/4 tsp ground turmeric
- 1/4 tsp ground ginger
- 1/8 tsp ground cumin
- 1 bay leaf
- 5 tbsps heavy whipping cream (optional)

Directions

- Cook tomatoes, zucchini, onion, garlic, cilantro, red bell pepper, basil, lime juice, and salt in hot butter for about 25 minutes before transferring it to a blender and blending it until the required smoothness is achieved.
- Cook milk, curry powder, turmeric, ginger, coconut butter, cumin, and bay leaf in the same pan for about 5 minutes or until you see that coconut butter has melted.
- At the very end, add blended vegetables into it and cook for five more minutes.

- Garnish with heavy cream before serving.

Serving: 5

Timing Information:

Preparation	Cooking	Total Time
15 mins	35 mins	50 mins

Nutritional Information:

Calories	310 kcal
Carbohydrates	22.9 g
Cholesterol	55 mg
Fat	22.4 g
Fiber	5.7 g
Protein	8.5 g
Sodium	147 mg

* Percent Daily Values are based on a 2,000 calorie diet.

Chicken Burgers Re-Imagined From Thailand

Ingredients

- 1 cup mayonnaise
- 1/4 cup flaked coconut, finely chopped
- 1 tbsp chopped fresh mint
- 2 pounds ground chicken
- 2 1/2 cups panko bread crumbs
- 1/2 cup Thai peanut sauce
- 2 tbsps red curry paste
- 2 tbsps minced green onion
- 2 tbsps minced fresh parsley
- 2 tsps soy sauce
- 3 cloves garlic, minced
- 2 tsps lemon juice
- 2 tsps lime juice
- 1 tbsp hot pepper sauce
- 8 hamburger buns, split and toasted

Directions

- At first you need to set a grill or grilling plate to medium heat and put some oil before starting anything else.
- Refrigerate a mixture of mayonnaise, mint and coconut for one hour.
- Combine ground chicken, Thai peanut sauce, curry paste, parsley, soy sauce, garlic, lemon juice, green onion, panko crumbs, lime juice, and hot pepper sauce in large sized bowl.
- Cook this on the preheated grill for about 8 minutes each side or until tender.
- Serve this with toasted bun.

NOTE: Adjust grilling times accordingly if using a grilling plate instead of a conventional grill.

Serving: 8

Timing Information:

Preparation	Cooking	Total Time
15 mins	15 mins	30 mins

Nutritional Information:

Calories	612 kcal
Carbohydrates	50.9 g
Cholesterol	80 mg
Fat	35.4 g
Fiber	2 g
Protein	36.5 g
Sodium	859 mg

* Percent Daily Values are based on a 2,000 calorie diet.

Classical Shrimp In Thailand

Ingredients

- 4 cloves garlic, peeled
- 1 (1 inch) piece fresh ginger root
- 1 fresh jalapeno pepper, seeded
- 1/2 tsp salt
- 1/2 tsp ground turmeric
- 2 tbsps vegetable oil
- 1 medium onion, diced
- 1 pound medium shrimp - peeled and deveined
- 2 tomatoes, seeded and diced
- 1 cup coconut milk
- 3 tbsps chopped fresh basil leaves

Directions

- Blend the mixture of garlic, turmeric, ginger and jalapeno in a blender until the required smoothness is achieved.
- Cook onion in hot oil for a few minutes before adding spice paste and cooking for another few minutes.
- Cook shrimp for a few minutes in it before adding tomatoes and coconut milk, and cooking it for five minutes covered with lid.
- Now cook for five more minutes without lid to get the sauce thick.
- Also add some fresh basil at the last minute.
- Serve.

Serving: 4

Timing Information:

Preparation	Cooking	Total Time
10 mins	20 mins	30 mins

Nutritional Information:

Calories	289 kcal
Carbohydrates	8.2 g
Cholesterol	173 mg
Fat	20.1 g
Fiber	2.1 g
Protein	20.9 g
Sodium	502 mg

* Percent Daily Values are based on a 2,000 calorie diet.

DELIGHTFULLY THAI BASIL CHICKEN

Ingredients

- 2 tbsps peanut oil
- 1/4 cup minced garlic
- 1 pound ground chicken breast
- 12 Thai chilis, sliced into thin rings
- 2 tsps black soy sauce
- 2 tbsps fish sauce
- 1 cup fresh basil leaves

Directions

- Cook garlic in hot peanut oil for about twenty seconds before adding ground chicken and cooking for another two minutes or until the chicken loses any pinkness.
- Now add sliced chilies, fish sauce and soy sauce into it before cooking for 15 seconds to get the chilies tender.
- At the very end, add basil and cook until you see that basil has wilted.
- Serve.

Serving: 4

Timing Information:

Preparation	Cooking	Total Time
15 mins	5 mins	20 mins

Nutritional Information:

Calories	273 kcal
Carbohydrates	16.5 g
Cholesterol	69 mg
Fat	10.7 g
Fiber	2.4 g
Protein	29.4 g
Sodium	769 mg

* Percent Daily Values are based on a 2,000 calorie diet.

A Pizza From Thailand

Ingredients

- 1 (12 inch) pre-baked pizza crust
- 1 (7 ounce) jar peanut sauce
- 1/4 cup peanut butter
- 8 ounces cooked skinless, boneless chicken breast halves, cut into strips
- 1 cup shredded Italian cheese blend
- 1 bunch green onions, chopped
- 1/2 cup fresh bean sprouts(optional)
- 1/2 cup shredded carrot(optional)
- 1 tbsp chopped roasted peanuts (optional)

Directions

- Preheat your oven to 400 degrees F.
- Spread a mixture of peanut sauce and peanut butter over the pizza crust and also put some strips of chicken, green onions and cheese.
- Bake in the preheated oven for about 12 minutes or until the cheese has melted.
- Garnish with carrot shreds, peanuts and sprouts.
- Serve.

Serving: 8

Timing Information:

Preparation	Cooking	Total Time
10 mins	10 mins	20 mins

Nutritional Information:

Calories	396 kcal
Carbohydrates	33.3 g
Cholesterol	37 mg
Fat	20.2 g
Fiber	3.3 g
Protein	24.2 g
Sodium	545 mg

* Percent Daily Values are based on a 2,000 calorie diet.

Spicy Thai Pasta

Ingredients

- 1 (12 ounce) package rice vermicelli
- 1 large tomato, diced
- 4 green onions, diced
- 2 pounds cooked shrimp, peeled and deveined
- 1 1/2 cups prepared Thai peanut sauce

Directions

- Add rice vermicelli into boiling water and cook for about five minutes or until done.
- Combine this rice with tomato, peanut sauce, green onions and shrimp very thoroughly in a medium sized bowl before refrigerating for at least eight hours.

•

Serving: 8

Timing Information:

Preparation	Cooking	Total Time
15 mins	5 mins	20 mins

Nutritional Information:

Calories	564 kcal
Carbohydrates	52.4 g
Cholesterol	230 mg
Fat	19.3 g
Fiber	4.3 g
Protein	46.3 g
Sodium	375 mg

* Percent Daily Values are based on a 2,000 calorie diet.

CHAPTER 4: INDONESIAN RECIPES
EASY INDONESIAN COOKBOOK

Indonesian Classical Satay

Ingredients

- 3 tbsps soy sauce
- 3 tbsps tomato sauce
- 1 tbsp peanut oil
- 2 cloves garlic, peeled and minced
- 1 pinch ground black pepper
- 1 pinch ground cumin
- 6 skinless, boneless chicken breast halves - cubed

- 1 tbsp vegetable oil
- 1/4 cup minced onion
- 1 clove garlic, peeled and minced
- 1 cup water
- 1/2 cup chunky peanut butter
- 2 tbsps soy sauce
- 2 tbsps white sugar
- 1 tbsp lemon juice
- skewers

Directions

- At first you need to set a grill or grilling plate to high heat and put some oil before starting anything else.
- Coat chicken with a mixture of soy sauce, cumin, tomato sauce, black pepper, peanut oil and garlic, and refrigerate it for at least 15 minutes.
- Cook onion and garlic in hot oil until brown before adding water, sugar, peanut butter and soy sauce into it.
- Add lemon juice after removing from heat.
- Thread all the chicken pieces into skewers
- Cook this on the preheated grill for about 5 minutes each side or until tender.
- Serve this with peanut sauce.

NOTE: If using a grilling plate please adjust the cooking time of the meat, to make sure that everything is cooked fully through.

NOTE: For peanut sauce recipe please see recipe for Satay Ayam.

NOTE: You will find that a few of these recipes call for a grill. Real Southeast Asian food is cooked street-style over an open flame, outside. For maximum authenticity use a grill.

Serving: 6

Timing Information:

Preparation	Cooking	Total Time
25 mins	20 mins	1 hr

Nutritional Information:

Calories	329 kcal
Carbohydrates	11.8 g
Cholesterol	67 mg
Fat	18.2 g
Fiber	2.2 g
Protein	30.8 g
Sodium	957 mg

* Percent Daily Values are based on a 2,000 calorie diet.

Pork Satay

Ingredients

- 2 cloves garlic
- 1/2 cup chopped green onions
- 1 tbsp chopped fresh ginger root
- 1 cup roasted, salted Spanish peanuts
- 2 tbsps lemon juice
- 2 tbsps honey
- 1/2 cup soy sauce
- 2 tsps crushed coriander seed
- 1 tsp red pepper flakes
- 1/2 cup chicken broth
- 1/2 cup melted butter
- 1 1/2 pounds pork tenderloin, cut into 1 inch cubes
- skewers

Directions

- At first you need to set a grill or grilling plate to medium heat and put some oil before starting anything else.
- Blend garlic, ginger, soy sauce, peanuts, lemon juice, honey, green onions, coriander, and red pepper flakes in a blender until you see that a smoothness is achieved.
- Coat pork cubes with this mixture by placing everything in a plastic bag and refrigerating for at least six hours.
- Thread pork cubes taken out from the bag onto skewers and boil the remaining marinade for about 5 minutes
- Cook this on the preheated grill for about 15 minutes each side or until tender, while brushing frequently with the cooked marinade.
- Serve with the remaining marinade.

NOTE: If using a grilling plate please adjust the cooking time of the meat, to make sure that everything is cooked fully through.

Serving: 4

Timing Information:

Preparation	Cooking	Total Time
30 mins	10 mins	6 hr 40 mins

Nutritional Information:

Calories	683 kcal
Carbohydrates	**22.1 g**
Cholesterol	156 mg
Fat	**49.7 g**
Fiber	**4.2 g**
Protein	**41.6 g**
Sodium	2332 mg

* Percent Daily Values are based on a 2,000 calorie diet.

Indo-Chinese Spiced Rice

Ingredients

- 3 tbsps vegetable oil
- 1 large onion, chopped
- 2 jalapeno peppers, seeded and minced
- 2 cloves garlic, crushed
- 1 tsp ground turmeric
- 1/2 tsp ground cinnamon
- 2 cups uncooked long-grain white rice
- 2 (14.5 ounce) cans chicken broth
- 1 cup water
- 1 bay leaf
- 2 green onions, chopped

Directions

- Cook onion, garlic and jalapeno peppers for about eight minutes before adding turmeric and cooking for two more minutes.
- Now add chicken broth, bay leaf and water, and cook all this for about 20 minutes after bringing this mixture to boil.
- Turn the heat off and let it stand as it is for about five minutes.
- Sprinkle some green onion over it before serving.

Serving: 8

Timing Information:

Preparation	Cooking	Total Time
10 mins	25 mins	35 mins

Nutritional Information:

Calories	226 kcal
Carbohydrates	39.8 g
Cholesterol	0 mg
Fat	5.5 g
Fiber	1.3 g
Protein	3.7 g
Sodium	4 mg

* Percent Daily Values are based on a 2,000 calorie diet.

NASI GORENG

(CHICKEN FRIED RICE DISH WITH SAUCE)

Ingredients

- 12 ounces long grain white rice
- 3 cups water
- salt to taste
- 2 tbsps sunflower seed oil
- 1 pound skinless, boneless chicken breast halves
- 2 cloves garlic, coarsely chopped
- 1 fresh red chile pepper, seeded and chopped
- 1 tbsp curry paste
- 1 bunch green onions, thinly sliced
- 2 tbsps soy sauce, or more to taste
- 1 tsp sunflower seed oil
- 2 eggs
- 2 ounces roasted peanuts, coarsely chopped
- 1/4 cup chopped fresh cilantro

Directions

- Bring a mixture of rice, water and salt to boil in a pan before turning down the heat to low and cooking for another 25 minutes to get the rice tender.
- Cook chicken, garlic and red chili pepper for about seven minutes before adding curry paste, cooked rice and green onion into it and cooking for another five minutes, while adding soy sauce at the end.
- Put the rice mixture aside; cook egg in the in a pot and when finished, mix it with the rice very thoroughly.
- Garnish with peanuts and cilantro before serving.

Serving: 6

Timing Information:

Preparation	Cooking	Total Time
15 mins	35 mins	50 mins

Nutritional Information:

Calories	430 kcal
Carbohydrates	51.5 g
Cholesterol	101 mg
Fat	13.8 g
Fiber	2.7 g
Protein	24.3 g
Sodium	491 mg

* Percent Daily Values are based on a 2,000 calorie diet.

Indonesian Inspired Ketchup

Ingredients

- 1 1/4 cups soy sauce
- 1 cup molasses (such as Grandma's®)
- 2 tbsps brown sugar
- 1 cube chicken bouillon (such as Knorr®)

Directions

- Mix all the ingredients mentioned above in a saucepan and cook it over low heat until you see that a slow boil is reached.
- Turn the heat off and cool it down.
- Store this in an airtight container and in a refrigerator.

Serving: 3

Timing Information:

Preparation	Cooking	Total Time
5 mins	15 mins	20 mins

Nutritional Information:

Calories	31 kcal
Carbohydrates	7.4 g
Cholesterol	< 1 mg
Fat	0 g
Fiber	0.1 g
Protein	0.5 g
Sodium	479 mg

* Percent Daily Values are based on a 2,000 calorie diet.

INDONESIAN FRIED RICE

Ingredients

- 1/2 cup uncooked long grain white rice
- 1 cup water
- 2 tsps sesame oil
- 1 small onion, chopped
- 2 cloves garlic, minced
- 1 green chile pepper, chopped
- 1 small carrot, sliced
- 1 stalk celery, sliced
- 2 tbsps kecap manis
- 2 tbsps tomato sauce
- 2 tbsps soy sauce
- 1/4 cucumber, sliced
- 4 eggs

Directions

- Bring a mixture of rice and water to boil before turning down the heat to low and cooking for 20 minutes.
- Cook onion, green chili and garlic in hot oil for a few minutes before adding carrot, rice, tomato sauce, celery, soy sauce and kecap manis, and cooking for another few minutes.
- Transfer this to a bowl, while garnishing with cucumber slices.
- Cook eggs in the pan and when done, put them over rice and vegetables.

Serving: 4

Timing Information:

Preparation	Cooking	Total Time
25 mins	15 mins	40 mins

Nutritional Information:

Calories	215 kcal
Carbohydrates	26.7 g
Cholesterol	186 mg
Fat	7.7 g
Fiber	1.6 g
Protein	10 g
Sodium	1033 mg

* Percent Daily Values are based on a 2,000 calorie diet.

Indo-Chinese Chicken

Ingredients

- 1 cup uncooked long grain white rice
- 2 cups water
- 1 pound fresh green beans, trimmed and snapped
- 2 tsps olive oil
- 1 pound skinless, boneless chicken breast halves - cut into chunks
- 3/4 cup low-sodium chicken broth
- 1/3 cup smooth peanut butter
- 2 tsps honey
- 1 tbsp low sodium soy sauce
- 1 tsp red chile paste
- 2 tbsps lemon juice
- 3 green onions, thinly sliced
- 2 tbsps chopped peanuts(optional)

Directions

- Bring a mixture of rice and water to boil before turning down the heat to low and cooking for 20 minutes.
- Put green beans in a steamer basket over boiling water and steam it for about ten minutes or until you find that it is tender.
- Cook chicken in hot oil for about five minutes on each side.
- Combine chicken broth, honey, soy sauce, peanut butter, chile paste and lemon juice in a pan, and cook it for about five minutes before adding green beans.
- Serve this over rice and garnish with green onions and peanuts.

Serving: 4

Timing Information:

Preparation	Cooking	Total Time
15 mins	30 mins	45 mins

Nutritional Information:

Calories	530 kcal
Carbohydrates	58.1 g
Cholesterol	59 mg
Fat	18.6 g
Fiber	6.4 g
Protein	35.4 g
Sodium	322 mg

* Percent Daily Values are based on a 2,000 calorie diet.

Mie Goreng

(Indonesian Fried Noodles)

Ingredients

- 3 (3 ounce) packages ramen noodles (without flavor packets)
- 1 tbsp vegetable oil
- 1 pound skinless, boneless chicken breast halves, cut into strips
- 1 tsp olive oil
- 1 tsp garlic salt
- 1 pinch ground black pepper, or to taste
- 1 tbsp vegetable oil
- 1/2 cup chopped shallots
- 5 cloves garlic, chopped
- 1 cup shredded cabbage
- 1 cup shredded carrots
- 1 cup broccoli florets
- 1 cup sliced fresh mushrooms
- 1/4 cup soy sauce
- 1/4 cup sweet soy sauce (Indonesian kecap manis)
- 1/4 cup oyster sauce
- salt and pepper to taste

Directions

- Cook noodles in boiling water for about 3 minutes before running it through cold water to stop the process of cooking and draining all the water.
- Coat chicken strips with olive oil, black pepper and garlic salt before cooking it in hot oil for about 5 minutes or until you see that the chicken is no longer pink.
- Now add garlic and shallots, and cook them until you see that they are turning brown.
- Now add all the vegetables into the pan and cook it for another five minutes or until you see that the vegetables are tender.
- Add the mixture of noodles, soy sauce, oyster sauce and sweet soy sauce into the pan containing chicken and vegetables.
- Sprinkle some salt and pepper before serving.
- Enjoy.

●

Serving: 6

Timing Information:

Preparation	Cooking	Total Time
15 mins	25 mins	40 mins

Nutritional Information:

Calories	356 kcal
Carbohydrates	34 g
Cholesterol	43 mg
Fat	14.3 g
Fiber	1.7 g
Protein	22.7 g
Sodium	1824 mg

* Percent Daily Values are based on a 2,000 calorie diet.

PISANG GORENG

(INDONESIAN BANANA FRITTERS I)

Ingredients

- 1 1/4 cups all-purpose flour
- 2 tbsps granulated sugar
- 1/4 tbsp vanilla powder
- 1/2 cup milk
- 1 egg
- 2 tbsps butter, melted
- 1 tsp rum flavoring
- 4 ripe bananas, sliced
- 2 cups oil for frying

Directions

- Mix flour, vanilla powder and sugar before making a space in the center and adding milk, melted butter, egg and rum flavoring.
- Combine it thoroughly before adding banana slices.
- Fry this banana mixture in hot oil for about 15 minutes or until golden brown.
- Remove these bananas from the oil and drain it well with the help of paper towels.
- Serve.

Serving: 4

Timing Information:

Preparation	Cooking	Total Time
5 mins	15 mins	20 mins

Nutritional Information:

Calories	489 kcal
Carbohydrates	73.2 g
Cholesterol	64 mg
Fat	19.5 g
Fiber	5 g
Protein	8.3 g
Sodium	73 mg

* Percent Daily Values are based on a 2,000 calorie diet.

Kecap Manis Sedang

(Indo-Chinese Soy Sauce)

Ingredients

- 2/3 cup soy sauce
- 1 cup water
- 2/3 cup brown sugar
- 8 bay leaves

Directions

- In a mixture of sugar, water and soy sauce in a saucepan, put bay leaves and bring all this to a boil.
- Now turn down the heat to medium and cook it for another 30 minutes.
- Let cool.

NOTE: This recipe is very important for multiple Indonesian and Indo-Chinese dishes mentioned throughout this cookbook.

Serving: 12

Timing Information:

Preparation	Cooking	Total Time
5 mins	15 mins	20 mins

Nutritional Information:

Calories	54 kcal
Carbohydrates	13.1 g
Cholesterol	0 mg
Fat	0 g
Fiber	0.1 g
Protein	0.9 g
Sodium	806 mg

* Percent Daily Values are based on a 2,000 calorie diet.

Satay Ayam

(Indo chicken with Peanut Sauce)

Ingredients

- 1 pound chicken thighs, cut into 1/2-inch pieces
- 3/4 tsp salt
- 1 pinch ground white pepper
- 1 tbsp sunflower seed oil
- 24 wooden skewers

Peanut Sauce:

- 1 cup water
- 5 tbsps peanut butter
- 2 tbsps kecap manis (sweet soy sauce)
- 1 tbsp brown sugar
- 2 cloves garlic, minced
- 1/2 tsp salt
- 1 tbsp lime juice

Directions

- Coat chicken thighs with ¾ tsp salt, sunflower seed oil and white pepper before refrigerating it for at least two hours.
- Bring a mixture of water, salt, peanut butter, kecap manis, garlic and brown sugar to boil before removing it from heat and adding some lime juice to make peanut sauce.
- Thread these chicken thighs onto skewers, while saving some marinade for later use.
- Cook these chicken thighs on a preheated grill for about 2 minutes each side or until tender.
- Serve this with peanut sauce.

NOTE: You can use a grilling plate as well for this recipe, just increase the cooking time of the meat. Use of a grill is preferred.

Serving: 4

Timing Information:

Preparation	Cooking	Total Time
10 mins	30 mins	40 mins

Nutritional Information:

Calories	326 kcal
Carbohydrates	8.9 g
Cholesterol	70 mg
Fat	21.8 g
Fiber	1.4 g
Protein	24.9 g
Sodium	1339 mg

* Percent Daily Values are based on a 2,000 calorie diet.

Skirt Steak

Ingredients

- 1 1/2 cups sweet soy sauce (Indonesian kecap manis)
- 1 cup sake
- 1 cup pineapple juice
- 1 cup mirin
- 1/2 cup reduced-sodium soy sauce
- 1/4 bunch fresh cilantro, chopped
- 1 tbsp white sugar
- 1 tbsp minced fresh ginger root
- 1 tbsp minced garlic
- 1 tbsp chopped scallions (green onions)
- 1 tbsp chili paste(optional)
- 1 (1 pound) skirt steak

Directions

- At first you need to set grill or grilling plate to medium heat and put some oil before starting anything else.
- Mix sweet soy sauce (kecap manis), scallions, sake, mirin, reduced-sodium soy sauce, cilantro, pineapple juice, sugar, ginger, garlic, and chili paste in large sized glass bowl before coating skirt steak with this mixture.
- Wrap it up with a plastic bag and marinate it for at least three hours.
- Remove every piece of meat from the marinade and cook this marinade in a saucepan for about 10 minutes over medium heat.
- Cook meat on the preheated grill for about 8 minutes each side or until tender.
- Serve it with the cooked marinade.

NOTE: If using a grilling plate please adjust the cooking time of the meat, to make sure that everything is cooked fully through.

Serving: 6

Timing Information:

Preparation	Cooking	Total Time
15 mins	20 mins	35 mins

Nutritional Information:

Calories	437 kcal
Carbohydrates	46.2 g
Cholesterol	27 mg
Fat	4.8 g
Fiber	1.4 g
Protein	22.5 g
Sodium	6517 mg

* Percent Daily Values are based on a 2,000 calorie diet.

Prawn Nasi Goreng

(Fried Rice and Shrimp In Sauce)

Ingredients

- 2 tbsps vegetable oil, divided
- 3 eggs, beaten
- 2 tbsps dark soy sauce
- 2 tbsps ketchup
- 1 tbsp brown sugar
- 1 tsp toasted sesame oil
- 1 tsp sweet chili sauce
- 1 zucchini, chopped
- 1 carrot, chopped
- 8 green onions, sliced
- 1 clove garlic, crushed
- 2 cups cooked rice
- 1/2 pound cooked prawns
- 2 tbsps fresh chives, chopped

Directions

- Cook egg in hot oil for about 30 seconds each side and cut it into smaller pieces after letting it cool down.
- Mix soy sauce, brown sugar, sesame oil, ketchup and chili sauce in a bowl, and set it aside for later use.
- Cook zucchini, green onions and carrot in hot oil for about three minutes before adding garlic, sauce mixture, rice and prawns.
- Turn the heat off and serve it by topping with eggs and sliced chives.

Serving: 2

Timing Information:

Preparation	Cooking	Total Time
20 mins	10 mins	30 mins

Nutritional Information:

Calories	664 kcal
Carbohydrates	67.7 g
Cholesterol	500 mg
Fat	25.5 g
Fiber	4 g
Protein	41 g
Sodium	1497 mg

* Percent Daily Values are based on a 2,000 calorie diet.

JEMPUT JUMPUT

(INDO BANANA FRITTERS II)

Ingredients

- 5/8 cup all-purpose flour
- 1 pinch salt
- 1 tsp baking powder
- 6 ripe bananas
- 3 tbsps white sugar
- oil for frying

Directions

- Add a mixture of baking powder, flour and salt slowly into mashed bananas and sugar, while stirring continuously.
- Drop this mixture with help of a spoon into hot oil and cook for about 8 minutes, while turning only once.
- Serve after draining with paper towels.

●

Serving: 18

Timing Information:

Preparation	Cooking	Total Time
10 mins	15 mins	25 mins

Nutritional Information:

Calories	491 kcal
Carbohydrates	14.4 g
Cholesterol	0 mg
Fat	49.1 g
Fiber	1.1 g
Protein	0.9 g
Sodium	49 mg

* Percent Daily Values are based on a 2,000 calorie diet.

CHICKEN & BROCCOLI

Ingredients

- 12 ounces boneless, skinless chicken breast halves, cut into bite-sized pieces
- 1 tbsp oyster sauce
- 2 tbsps dark soy sauce
- 3 tbsps vegetable oil
- 2 cloves garlic, chopped
- 1 large onion, cut into rings
- 1/2 cup water
- 1 tsp ground black pepper
- 1 tsp white sugar
- 1/2 medium head bok choy, chopped
- 1 small head broccoli, chopped
- 1 tbsp cornstarch, mixed with equal parts water

Directions

- Mix chicken, soy sauce and oyster sauce in large bowl and set it aside for later use.
- Cook garlic and onion in hot oil for about three minutes before adding chicken mixture and cooking it for another ten minutes.
- Now add water, sugar, broccoli, pepper and bok choy, and cook it for another ten minutes.
- In the end, add cornstarch mixture and cook it for another 5 minutes to get the sauce thick.
- Enjoy.

Serving: 6

Timing Information:

Preparation	Cooking	Total Time
10 mins	25 mins	35 mins

Nutritional Information:

Calories	170 kcal
Carbohydrates	9.8 g
Cholesterol	33 mg
Fat	7.9 g
Fiber	2.5 g
Protein	16.2 g
Sodium	418 mg

* Percent Daily Values are based on a 2,000 calorie diet.

INDO-CHINESE SATE

(MEAT KABOBS)

Ingredients

- 1 onion, chopped
- 1 clove garlic, minced
- 1 1/2 tbsps kecap manis
- 1 tsp ground coriander
- 1 tsp ground cumin
- 1 tsp sambal oelek (sriracha sauce)
- 1/2 cup red wine
- 1 1/2 tbsps water
- 1 lemon grass, bruised, and cut into 1 inch pieces
- 1 pound sirloin steak, cut into 1-inch cubes

Directions

- At first you need to set a grill or grilling plate to medium heat and put some oil before starting anything else.
- Blend onion, garlic, coriander, cumin, kecap manis, sambal oelek, red wine and water in a blender until smooth before adding lemon grass and coating beef with this marinade.
- Wrap it up with a plastic bag and refrigerate it for at least two hours.
- Thread these beef pieces onto the skewers.
- Cook this on the preheated grill for about 5 minutes each side or until tender.

NOTE: If using a grilling plate please adjust the cooking time of the meat, to make sure that everything is cooked fully through.

Serving: 4

Timing Information:

Preparation	Cooking	Total Time
15 mins	5 mins	2 hr 20 mins

Nutritional Information:

Calories	200 kcal
Carbohydrates	**6.5 g**
Cholesterol	69 mg
Fat	**5.4 g**
Fiber	**0.9 g**
Protein	**25.1 g**
Sodium	419 mg

* Percent Daily Values are based on a 2,000 calorie diet.

Telur Balado

(Spicy Indonesian Eggs)

Ingredients

- 1 cup vegetable oil for frying
- 6 hard-boiled eggs, shells removed
- 6 red chili peppers, seeded and chopped
- 4 cloves garlic
- 4 medium shallots
- 2 tomatoes, quartered
- 1 tsp shrimp paste
- 1 1/2 tbsps peanut oil
- 1 tbsp vegetable oil
- 1 tsp white vinegar
- 1 tsp white sugar
- salt and pepper to taste

Directions

- Deep fry eggs in a pan for about seven minutes over medium heat or until golden brown in color.
- Put chili peppers, shallots, garlic, tomatoes, and shrimp in a blender until you see that the required smoothness is achieved.
- Cook chili pepper mixture in hot oil before adding vinegar, pepper, sugar, fried eggs and salt into a mixture.
- Turn down the heat to medium and cook it for about 5 minutes, while turning it frequently.
- Serve.

Serving: 6

Timing Information:

Preparation	Cooking	Total Time
15 mins	20 mins	35 mins

Nutritional Information:

Calories	237 kcal
Carbohydrates	13.1 g
Cholesterol	201 mg
Fat	17.3 g
Fiber	1.4 g
Protein	9.1 g
Sodium	115 mg

* Percent Daily Values are based on a 2,000 calorie diet.

Ayam Masak Merah

(Spicy Tomato Chicken)

Ingredients

- 1 (3 pound) whole chicken, cut into 8 pieces
- 1 tsp ground turmeric
- salt to taste
- 1/4 cup dried red chili peppers
- 3 fresh red chili pepper, finely chopped
- 4 cloves garlic, minced
- 1 red onion, chopped
- 1 (3/4 inch thick) slice fresh ginger root
- 2 tbsps sunflower seed oil
- 1 cinnamon stick
- 2 whole star anise pods
- 5 whole cloves
- 5 cardamom seeds
- 2 tomatoes, sliced
- 2 tbsps ketchup
- 1 tsp white sugar, or to taste
- 1/2 cup water
-

Directions

- Coat chicken with turmeric powder and salt, and set it aside for later use.
- Put dried red chili peppers in hot water until you see that it is soft.
- Put softened dried chili, garlic, fresh red chili peppers, onion, and ginger in a blender and blend it until you get a paste.
- Cook chicken in hot oil until you see that it is golden from all sides and set it aside.
- Now cook chili paste, cinnamon, cardamom seeds, star anise,

and cloves in the same pan for few minutes before adding chicken and water into it.

- Add tomatoes, sugar and ketchup, and bring all this to a boil before turning down the heat to medium and cooking for another 15 minutes.
- Serve.

Serving: 4

Timing Information:

Preparation	Cooking	Total Time
20 mins	35 mins	55 mins

Nutritional Information:

Calories	462 kcal
Carbohydrates	15.4 g
Cholesterol	92 mg
Fat	29.7 g
Fiber	3.3 g
Protein	33.6 g
Sodium	183 mg

* Percent Daily Values are based on a 2,000 calorie diet.

CAP CAI

(INDO-CHINESE SHRIMP VEGGIE SALAD)

Ingredients

- 3 tbsps vegetable oil
- 4 cloves garlic, minced
- 1 onion, thinly sliced
- 10 ounces peeled and deveined medium shrimp (30-40 per pound)
- 1 head bok choy, chopped
- 1 1/2 cups chopped broccoli
- 1 1/2 cups chopped cauliflower
- 1 large carrot, thinly sliced at an angle
- 3 green onions, chopped
- 2/3 cup water
- 2 tbsps cornstarch
- 2 tbsps fish sauce
- 2 tbsps oyster sauce
- 1 tsp white sugar
- 1/2 tsp ground black pepper
- salt to taste

Directions

- Cook onion and garlic in hot oil for about five minutes before adding shrimp, broccoli, cauliflower, bok choy, carrot, water and green onion, and cook this for about 15 minutes or until you see that all the vegetables are tender.
- Add a mixture of fish sauce and cornstarch, to the cap cai and also some oyster sauce, pepper and sugar.
- Mix it thoroughly and add some salt according to your taste before serving.

Serving: 4

Timing Information:

Preparation	Cooking	Total Time
20 mins	25 mins	45 mins

Nutritional Information:

Calories	250 kcal
Carbohydrates	18.7 g
Cholesterol	106 mg
Fat	11.9 g
Fiber	4.4 g
Protein	18.9 g
Sodium	819 mg

* Percent Daily Values are based on a 2,000 calorie diet.

CHAPTER 5: VIETNAMESE RECIPES
EASY VIETNAMESE COOKBOOK

CHICKEN MEATBALLS IN VIETNAM

Ingredients

- 1 1/2 pounds ground chicken
- 1 clove garlic, minced
- 1 egg white
- 1 tbsp rice wine
- 2 tbsps soy sauce
- 1/2 tsp Worcestershire sauce
- 2 tsps fish sauce
- 1/2 tsp white sugar
- salt and white pepper to taste
- 2 tbsps cornstarch
- 1 tbsp sesame oil

Directions

- Preheat the broiler of your oven before doing anything else.
- Combine ground chicken, Worcestershire sauce, sugar, garlic, rice wine, soy sauce, egg white, fish sauce, salt, pepper, corn starch and sesame oil in a medium sized bowl before forming small balls out of it and threading them onto skewers.
- Put these skewers on a baking sheet.
- Broil it for 20 minutes or until you see that it is cooked.

Serving: 6

Timing Information:

Preparation	Cooking	Total Time
20 mins	35 mins	55 mins

Nutritional Information:

Calories	184 kcal
Carbohydrates	4.1 g
Cholesterol	69 mg
Fat	5.9 g
Fiber	0.1 g
Protein	26.5 g
Sodium	497 mg

* Percent Daily Values are based on a 2,000 calorie diet.

SPRING ROLLS VIETNAMESE STYLE

Ingredients

- 2 ounces rice vermicelli
- 8 rice wrappers (8.5 inch diameter)
- 8 large cooked shrimp - peeled, deveined and cut in half
- 1 1/3 tbsps chopped fresh Thai basil
- 3 tbsps chopped fresh mint leaves
- 3 tbsps chopped fresh cilantro
- 2 leaves lettuce, chopped
- 4 tsps fish sauce
- 1/4 cup water
- 2 tbsps fresh lime juice
- 1 clove garlic, minced
- 2 tbsps white sugar
- 1/2 tsp garlic chili sauce
- 3 tbsps hoisin sauce
- 1 tsp finely chopped peanuts

Directions

- Cook rice vermicelli in boiling water for five minutes or until done and then drain.
- Dip a rice wrapper in hot water for one second to soften it up before placing shrimp halves, basil, mint, vermicelli, cilantro and lettuce, and then roll this wrapper around these things.
- Mix fish sauce, lime juice, garlic, water, sugar and chili sauce in a small bowl before mixing peanuts and hoisin sauce in a separate bowl.
- Serve spring roll with these two sauces.

Serving: 8

Timing Information:

Preparation	Cooking	Total Time
45 mins	5 mins	50 mins

Nutritional Information:

Calories	82 kcal
Carbohydrates	15.8 g
Cholesterol	11 mg
Fat	0.7 g
Fiber	0.6 g
Protein	3.3 g
Sodium	305 mg

* Percent Daily Values are based on a 2,000 calorie diet.

A Vietnamese Inspired Chicken Salad

Ingredients

- 1 tbsp finely chopped green chile peppers
- 1 tbsp rice vinegar
- 2 tbsps fresh lime juice
- 3 tbsps Asian fish sauce
- 3 cloves garlic, minced
- 1 tbsp white sugar
- 1 tbsp Asian (toasted) sesame oil
- 2 tbsps vegetable oil
- 1 tsp black pepper
- 2 cooked skinless boneless chicken breast halves, shredded
- 1/2 head cabbage, cored and thinly sliced
- 1 carrot, cut into matchsticks
- 1/3 onion, finely chopped
- 1/3 cup finely chopped dry roasted peanuts
- 1/3 cup chopped fresh cilantro

Directions

- Combine chopped green chilies, sesame oil, lime juice, fish sauce, garlic, sugar, rice vinegar, vegetable oil and black pepper in a medium sized bowl very thoroughly so that the sugar is completely dissolved.
- Mix chicken, carrot, onion, peanuts, cabbage and cilantro in a separate bowl.
- Pour the bowl containing dressing over this and serve it after thoroughly mixing it.

•

Serving: 4

Timing Information:

Preparation	Cooking	Total Time
30 mins		30 mins

Nutritional Information:

Calories	303 kcal
Carbohydrates	19.3 g
Cholesterol	37 mg
Fat	17.9 g
Fiber	5.7 g
Protein	19.2 g
Sodium	991 mg

* Percent Daily Values are based on a 2,000 calorie diet.

Lamb Chops In Vietnam

Ingredients

- 15 (3 ounce) lamb loin chops (1-inch thick) lamb loin chops (1-inch thick)
- 2 cloves garlic, sliced
- 1 tsp garlic powder, or to taste
- 1 pinch chili powder
- 2 tbsps white sugar
- freshly ground black pepper to taste
- 1 tbsp fresh lime juice
- 1 tbsp soy sauce
- 2 tbsps olive oil
- 1/4 cup chopped fresh cilantro
- 2 lime wedges
- 2 lemon wedges

Directions

- Set your oven at 400 degrees F before doing anything else.
- Add the garlic, garlic powder, sugar, salt, lime juice, chili powder, soy sauce, olive oil and pepper in a roasting pan over lamb chops.
- Bake this in the preheated oven for about 30 minutes or until tender before garnishing it with cilantro and adding some lime juice.
- Serve.

Serving: 5

Timing Information:

Preparation	Cooking	Total Time
10 mins	20 mins	8 hr 30 mins

Nutritional Information:

Calories	555 kcal
Carbohydrates	**7.4 g**
Cholesterol	151 mg
Fat	**40.4 g**
Fiber	**0.6 g**
Protein	**38.6 g**
Sodium	301 mg

* Percent Daily Values are based on a 2,000 calorie diet.

A Southeast Asian Pork I

Ingredients

- 1 tbsp vegetable oil
- 1 cup white sugar
- 2 pounds pork spareribs, cut into 1-inch pieces
- 2 green onions, cut in 2-inch lengths
- 1 green chili pepper, chopped
- 1 tsp ground black pepper
- 2 shallots, finely chopped
- 2 cloves garlic, minced
- salt to taste
- 1 tsp Asian (toasted) sesame oil
- 1 tbsp green onion, thinly sliced and separated into rings

Directions

- Cook sugar in hot oil in a skillet until you see that it is turning brown in color before adding pork, 2 green onions, black pepper, chili pepper, shallots, garlic, and salt, and mixing all this very thoroughly in the caramelized sugar.
- After the pork turns golden brown; add sesame oil and vegetables into it before turning down the heat to low and cooking it for a few minutes.
- When you see that juices have been absorbed then turn up the heat to high and cook all this for five minutes or until you see that the sauce is thick enough.
- Garnish this with some green onion rings.
- Serve

Serving: 4

Timing Information:

Preparation	Cooking	Total Time
15 mins	20 mins	35 mins

Nutritional Information:

Calories	657 kcal
Carbohydrates	56.8 g
Cholesterol	120 mg
Fat	34.7 g
Fiber	0.7 g
Protein	29.9 g
Sodium	98 mg

* Percent Daily Values are based on a 2,000 calorie diet.

PHO SOUP

Ingredients

- 2 (14.5 ounce) cans chicken broth
- 2 star anise pods, or more to taste
- 3/4 tbsp ginger paste
- 1 tsp sriracha hot sauce, or more to taste
- 4 ounces tofu, cubed
- 1/2 cup broccoli florets
- 1/2 cup sliced mushrooms
- 1/4 cup chopped carrots
- 1/2 (8 ounce) package dried thin rice noodles
- 1 tbsp chopped green onion

Directions

- Bring the mixture of chicken broth, ginger paste, star anise and sriracha hot sauce to boil before adding carrots, tofu, mushrooms and broccoli, and cooking it for seven minutes or until you see that the vegetables are tender.
- Put noodles in hot water for about four minutes and drain.
- After removing star anise from the broth mixture, add this mixture on top of noodles in serving bowls.
- Serve.

Serving: 4

Timing Information:

Preparation	Cooking	Total Time
15 mins	10 mins	25 mins

Nutritional Information:

Calories	159 kcal
Carbohydrates	29.2 g
Cholesterol	5 mg
Fat	2.3 g
Fiber	1.7 g
Protein	5.2 g
Sodium	991 mg

* Percent Daily Values are based on a 2,000 calorie diet.

Southeast Asian Pork II

Ingredients

- 4 pounds pork shoulder, cut into cubes
- 1 tsp salt
- 1 tsp ground black pepper
- 1/4 cup olive oil
- 2 cloves garlic, minced
- 2 tbsps brown sugar
- 2 tbsps soy sauce
- 1 tbsp fish sauce
- 1 tsp Chinese five-spice powder

Directions

- Cook garlic and pork that is seasoned with salt and pepper in hot oil for about ten minutes or until you see that pork is browned.
- Now add brown sugar, five-spice powder, soy sauce and fish sauce into the pork before turning down the heat to low and cooking it for 2 full hours or until you see that pork is tender.
- Serve.

Serving: 4

Timing Information:

Preparation	Cooking	Total Time
10 mins	2 hr 20 mins	2 hr 30 mins

Nutritional Information:

Calories	288 kcal
Carbohydrates	**4.4 g**
Cholesterol	85 mg
Fat	**16.4 g**
Fiber	**0.1 g**
Protein	**29.5**
Sodium	713 mg

* Percent Daily Values are based on a 2,000 calorie diet.

Easy Vietnamese Inspired Stir-Fry

Ingredients

- 1/4 cup olive oil
- 4 cloves garlic, minced
- 1 (1 inch) piece fresh ginger root, minced
- 1/4 cup fish sauce
- 1/4 cup reduced-sodium soy sauce
- 1 dash sesame oil
- 2 pounds sirloin tip, thinly sliced
- 1 tbsp vegetable oil
- 2 cloves garlic, minced
- 3 green onions, cut into 2 inch pieces
- 1 large onion, thinly sliced
- 2 cups frozen whole green beans, partially thawed
- 1/2 cup reduced-sodium beef broth
- 2 tbsps lime juice
- 1 tbsp chopped fresh Thai basil
- 1 tbsp chopped fresh mint
- 1 pinch red pepper flakes, or to taste
- 1/2 tsp ground black pepper
- 1/4 cup chopped fresh cilantro

Directions

- Add a mixture of olive oil, ginger, fish sauce, 4 cloves of garlic, soy sauce, and sesame oil into a plastic bag containing beef sirloin tips and shake it well to get beef coated with the mixture.
- Refrigerate it for at least two straight hours before removing the beef from the marinade.
- Cook this beef in hot oil for about seven minutes or until you see that it is no longer pink before setting it aside on a plate.
- Turn down the heat to medium and cook garlic, onion and green

onion for about five minutes before adding green beans, lime juice, basil, mint, beef broth, red pepper flakes, pepper and also the beef.

- Mix it thoroughly before adding cilantro.

Serving: 5

Timing Information:

Preparation	Cooking	Total Time
20 mins	30 mins	2 hr 50 mins

Nutritional Information:

Calories	475 kcal
Carbohydrates	**8.8 g**
Cholesterol	101 mg
Fat	**34.4 g**
Fiber	2 g
Protein	**31.7 g**
Sodium	1174 mg

* Percent Daily Values are based on a 2,000 calorie diet.

SHRIMP SOUP

Ingredients

- 1 tbsp vegetable oil
- 2 tsps minced fresh garlic
- 2 tsps minced fresh ginger root
- 1 (10 ounce) package frozen chopped spinach, thawed and drained
- salt and black pepper to taste
- 2 quarts chicken stock
- 1 cup shrimp stock
- 1 tsp hot pepper sauce(optional)
- 1 tsp hoisin sauce(optional)
- 20 peeled and deveined medium shrimp
- 1 (6.75 ounce) package long rice noodles (rice vermicelli)
- 2 green onions, chopped(optional)

Directions

- Cook garlic and ginger for about one minute before adding spinach, pepper and salt, and cooking it for 3 more minutes to get the spinach tender.
- Add chicken stock, hoisin sauce, shrimp stock and hot pepper sauce, and cook this for a few more minutes.
- In the end, add noodles and shrimp into it, and cook it for 4 minutes before adding green onions cooking it for another five minutes.
- Add salt and pepper according to your taste before serving.
- Enjoy.

●

Serving: 6

Timing Information:

Preparation	Cooking	Total Time
15 mins	20 mins	40 mins

Nutritional Information:

Calories	212 kcal
Carbohydrates	28.6 g
Cholesterol	52 mg
Fat	4.7 g
Fiber	2.7 g
Protein	14.4 g
Sodium	1156 mg

* Percent Daily Values are based on a 2,000 calorie diet.

Chinese Pork Chops

Ingredients

- 2 tbsps brown sugar
- 2 tbsps honey
- 2 tbsps fish sauce
- 3 tbsps vegetable oil
- 2 tbsps soy sauce
- 1/2 tsp Worcestershire sauce
- 1/2 tsp minced fresh ginger root
- 1 tsp Chinese five-spice powder
- 1 tsp sesame oil
- 1 tsp minced shallot
- 6 cloves garlic, minced
- 1/2 onion, chopped
- 2 lemon grass, chopped
- 1/4 tsp salt
- 1/2 tsp ground black pepper
- 6 thin, boneless center-cut pork chops
- 1/4 cup vegetable oil

Directions

- Add the mixture brown sugar, honey, lemon grass, soy sauce, Worcestershire sauce, ginger, five-spice powder, sesame oil, fish sauce, shallot, garlic, onion, vegetable oil, salt, and pepper into a plastic bag containing pork chops, and mix it well to coat pork chops thoroughly before refrigerating it for at least eight hours.
- Cook these pork chops on a preheated grill that is lightly oiled for about four minutes each side.
- Serve.

Serving: 6

Timing Information:

Preparation	Cooking	Total Time
15 mins	10 mins	8 hr 25 mins

Nutritional Information:

Calories	416 kcal
Carbohydrates	15 g
Cholesterol	63 mg
Fat	**28.8 g**
Fiber	**0.3 g**
Protein	**24.5 g**
Sodium	814 mg

* Percent Daily Values are based on a 2,000 calorie diet.

Tofu Based Salad In Vietnam

Ingredients

- 1 tbsp vegetable oil
- 2 tbsps chopped garlic
- 1 (14 ounce) package tofu, drained and cubed
- 1/2 cup peanuts
- 2 tbsps soy sauce
- 2 large cucumbers, peeled and thinly sliced
- 1/2 cup Vietnamese sweet chili sauce
- 1/4 cup lime juice
- 1 bunch chopped cilantro leaves

Directions

- Cook garlic in hot oil for about thirty seconds before adding tofu and peanuts, and cooking it again until tofu is lightly brown.
- Now add soy sauce and cook until you see that it is completely absorbed before refrigerating it for at least one hour.
- In the mixture of chili sauce, cilantro, sliced cucumbers and lime juice add tofu, and mix it thoroughly before serving.
- Enjoy.

Serving: 6

Timing Information:

Preparation	Cooking	Total Time
15 mins	25 mins	1 hr 40 mins

Nutritional Information:

Calories	200 kcal
Carbohydrates	**18.4 g**
Cholesterol	0 mg
Fat	**11.7 g**
Fiber	**2.6 g**
Protein	**9.5 g**
Sodium	636 mg

* Percent Daily Values are based on a 2,000 calorie diet.

Beef and Lettuce

Ingredients

- 1 cup uncooked long grain white rice
- 2 cups water
- 5 tsps white sugar
- 1 clove garlic, minced
- 1/4 cup fish sauce
- 5 tbsps water
- 1 1/2 tbsps chili sauce
- 1 lemon, juiced
- 2 tbsps vegetable oil
- 3 cloves garlic, minced
- 1 pound ground beef
- 1 tbsp ground cumin
- 1 (28 ounce) can canned diced tomatoes
- 2 cups lettuce leaves, torn into 1/2 inch wide strips

Directions

- Bring the water containing rice to boil before turning down the heat to low and cooking for 25 minutes.
- Add mashed sugar and garlic to the mixture of chili sauce, fish sauce, lemon juice and water in a medium sized bowl.
- Cook garlic in hot oil before adding beef and cumin, and cooking all this until you see that it is brown.
- Now add half of that fish sauce mixture and tomatoes into the pan, and after turning down the heat to low, cook all this for twenty more minutes.
- Add lettuce into this beef mixture before serving this over the cooked rice along with that remaining fish sauce.

Serving: 6

Timing Information:

Preparation	Cooking	Total Time
15 mins	45 mins	1 hr

Nutritional Information:

Calories	529 kcal
Carbohydrates	56.9 g
Cholesterol	69 mg
Fat	21 g
Fiber	4 g
Protein	26.3 g
Sodium	1481 mg

* Percent Daily Values are based on a 2,000 calorie diet.

Rice-Noodle Salad

Ingredients

- 5 cloves garlic
- 1 cup loosely packed chopped cilantro
- 1/2 jalapeno pepper, seeded and minced
- 3 tbsps white sugar
- 1/4 cup fresh lime juice
- 3 tbsps vegetarian fish sauce
- 1 (12 ounce) package dried rice noodles
- 2 carrots, julienned
- 1 cucumber, halved lengthwise and chopped
- 1/4 cup chopped fresh mint
- 4 leaves napa cabbage
- 1/4 cup unsalted peanuts
- 4 sprigs fresh mint

Directions

- Add a mashed mixture of hot pepper, garlic and cilantro into the bowl containing mixture of lime juice, sugar and fish sauce before letting it stand for at least five minutes.
- Cook rice noodles in boiling salty water for two minutes before draining it and passing it through cold water to stop the process of cooking.
- Mix sauce, carrots, cucumber, noodles, mint and Napa in large sized serving bowl very thoroughly before garnishing it with peanuts and mint sprigs.

•

Serving: 4

Timing Information:

Preparation	Cooking	Total Time
15 mins		15 mins

Nutritional Information:

Calories	432 kcal
Carbohydrates	89.5 g
Cholesterol	0 mg
Fat	5.3 g
Fiber	4.1 g
Protein	6.6 g
Sodium	188 mg

* Percent Daily Values are based on a 2,000 calorie diet.

CHICKEN WINGS IN VIETNAM

Ingredients

- 12 chicken wings, tips removed and wings cut in half at joint
- 2 cloves garlic, peeled and coarsely chopped
- 1/2 onion, cut into chunks
- 1/4 cup soy sauce
- 1/4 cup Asian fish sauce
- 2 tbsps fresh lemon juice
- 2 tbsps sesame oil
- 1 tsp salt
- 1 tsp freshly ground black pepper
- 1 tbsp garlic powder
- 1 tbsp white sugar

Directions

- Into the mixture of chicken wings, onion and garlic in large sized bowl; add fish sauce, sesame oi, salt, sugar, garlic powder, pepper and lemon juice before refrigerating it covered for at least two hours.
- Preheat your oven at 400 degrees F and place aluminum foil in the baking dish.
- Reserving some marinade for brushing; place all the wings on the baking dish and bake it for about 30 minutes or until you see that these have turned golden brown.

-

Serving: 4

Timing Information:

Preparation	Cooking	Total Time
15 mins	30 mins	2 hr 45 mins

Nutritional Information:

Calories	716 kcal
Carbohydrates	**9.1 g**
Cholesterol	213 mg
Fat	**50.9 g**
Fiber	**0.8 g**
Protein	53 g
Sodium	2781 mg

* Percent Daily Values are based on a 2,000 calorie diet.

BEEF PHO

Ingredients

- 4 quarts beef broth
- 1 large onion, sliced into rings
- 6 slices fresh ginger root
- 1 lemon grass
- 1 cinnamon stick
- 1 tsp whole black peppercorns
- 1 pound sirloin tip, cut into thin slices
- 1/2 pound bean sprouts
- 1 cup fresh basil leaves
- 1 cup fresh mint leaves
- 1 cup loosely packed cilantro leaves
- 3 fresh jalapeno peppers, sliced into rings
- 2 limes, cut into wedges
- 2 (8 ounce) packages dried rice noodles
- 1/2 tbsp hoisin sauce
- 1 dash hot pepper sauce
- 3 tbsps fish sauce

Directions

- Bring the mixture of broth, onion, lemon grass, cinnamon, ginger and peppercorns to boil before turning down the heat to low and cooking it for about one hour.
- Place bean sprouts, basil, cilantro, chilies, mint and lime on a platter very neatly.
- Place noodles in hot water for about 15 minutes before placing it in six different bowls evenly.
- Put raw beef over it before pouring in hot broth.
- Serve it with the platter and sauces.

Serving: 6

Timing Information:

Preparation	Cooking	Total Time
10 mins	1 hr 20 mins	1 hr 30 mins

Nutritional Information:

Calories	528 kcal
Carbohydrates	**73.1 g**
Cholesterol	51 mg
Fat	**13.6 g**
Fiber	**3.9 g**
Protein	**27.1 g**
Sodium	2844 mg

* Percent Daily Values are based on a 2,000 calorie diet.

A Chicken & Curry Soup from Southeast Asia

Ingredients

- 2 tbsps vegetable oil
- 1 (3 pound) whole chicken, skin removed and cut into pieces
- 1 onion, cut into chunks
- 2 shallots, thinly sliced
- 2 cloves garlic, chopped
- 1/8 cup thinly sliced fresh ginger root
- 1 stalk lemon grass, cut into 2 inch pieces
- 4 tbsps curry powder
- 1 green bell pepper, cut into 1 inch pieces
- 2 carrots, sliced diagonally
- 1 quart chicken broth
- 1 quart water
- 2 tbsps fish sauce
- 2 kaffir lime leaves
- 1 bay leaf
- 2 tsps red pepper flakes
- 8 small potatoes, quartered
- 1 (14 ounce) can coconut milk
- 1 bunch fresh cilantro

Directions

- Cook onion and chicken in hot oil until you see that onions are soft and then set it aside for later use.
- Cook shallots in the same pan for one minute before adding garlic, lemon grass, ginger and curry powder, and cooking it for another five minutes.
- Add pepper and carrots before stirring in chicken, onion, fish sauce, chicken broth and water.
- Also add lime leaves, red pepper flakes and bay leaf before bringing all this to boil and adding potatoes.
- Add coconut milk and cook it for 60 minutes after turning down the

heat to low.
- Garnish with a sprig of fresh cilantro.
- Serve.

Serving: 8

Timing Information:

Preparation	Cooking	Total Time
30 mins	2 hr	2 hr 30 mins

Nutritional Information:

Calories	512 kcal
Carbohydrates	**40.6 g**
Cholesterol	75 mg
Fat	**26.8 g**
Fiber	**6.7 g**
Protein	**29.8 g**
Sodium	374 mg

* Percent Daily Values are based on a 2,000 calorie diet.

A Vietnamese Condiment

Ingredients

- 1/4 cup white sugar
- 1/2 cup warm water
- 1/4 cup fish sauce
- 1/3 cup distilled white vinegar
- 1/2 lemon, juiced
- 3 cloves garlic, minced
- 3 Thai chile peppers, chopped
- 1 green onion, thinly sliced

Directions

- In a mixture of warm water and sugar; add fish sauce, garlic, green onion, lemon juice, vinegar and chili pepper.
- Mix all this very thoroughly before serving.
- Enjoy.

NOTE: Use this condiment for dipping spring rolls in, or as a topping for jasmine rice.

Serving: 5

Timing Information:

Preparation	Cooking	Total Time
15 mins		15 mins

Nutritional Information:

Calories	15 kcal
Carbohydrates	3.7 g
Cholesterol	0 mg
Fat	0 g
Fiber	0.3 g
Protein	0.4 g
Sodium	220 mg

* Percent Daily Values are based on a 2,000 calorie diet.

La Sa Ga

(A Vietnamese Soup)

Ingredients

- 3 tbsps peanut oil
- 1 cup diced onion
- 3 tbsps minced garlic
- 1 cup coconut milk, divided
- 1 tbsp red curry paste, or more to taste
- 2 cooked chicken breast halves, shredded
- 8 cups chicken stock
- 6 tbsps soy sauce, or to taste
- 1/4 cup fish sauce, or to taste
- 1 1/2 pounds angel hair pasta
- 1/4 cup chopped fresh basil, or to taste

Directions

- Cook onion and garlic in hot oil for about four minutes before adding coconut milk and stirring it continuously for about two minutes.
- Now add curry paste and stir it well for about two more minutes.
- Introduce chicken stock into the pan and cook it for about four minutes after turning up the heat to medium.
- Cook it for another four minutes after adding the remaining coconut milk.
- Stir in angel hair pasta before covering up the pot and cooking it for ten more minutes.
- Add basil before serving.

Serving: 8

Timing Information:

Preparation	Cooking	Total Time
20 mins	20 mins	40 mins

Nutritional Information:

Calories	333 kcal
Carbohydrates	41.8 g
Cholesterol	15 mg
Fat	13.5 g
Fiber	3.1 g
Protein	15.1 g
Sodium	1710 mg

* Percent Daily Values are based on a 2,000 calorie diet.

LEMON GRASS CHICKEN

Ingredients

- 2 tbsps vegetable oil
- 1 lemon grass, minced
- 1 (3 pound) whole chicken, cut into pieces
- 2/3 cup water
- 1 tbsp fish sauce
- 1 1/2 tbsps curry powder
- 1 tbsp cornstarch
- 1 tbsp chopped cilantro(optional)

Directions

- Cook lemon grass in hot oil for about 5 minutes before adding chicken and cooking it until you see that the chicken is no longer pink from the center.
- Now add fish sauce, curry powder and water into the pan before turning the heat up to high and cooking it for another 15 minutes.
- Now add the mixture of curry sauce and cornstarch into the pan, and cook all this for another five minutes.
- Garnish with cilantro before serving.

Serving: 4

Timing Information:

Preparation	Cooking	Total Time
15 mins	25 mins	40 mins

Nutritional Information:

Calories	813 kcal
Carbohydrates	4.6 g
Cholesterol	255 mg
Fat	58.4 g
Fiber	0.8 g
Protein	63.8 g
Sodium	515 mg

* Percent Daily Values are based on a 2,000 calorie diet.

A Sandwich In Vietnam

Ingredients

- 4 boneless pork loin chops, cut 1/4 inch thick
- 4 (7 inch) French bread baguettes, split lengthwise
- 4 tsps mayonnaise, or to taste
- 1 ounce chili sauce with garlic
- 1/4 cup fresh lime juice
- 1 small red onion, sliced into rings
- 1 medium cucumber, peeled and sliced lengthwise
- 2 tbsps chopped fresh cilantro
- salt and pepper to taste

Directions

- Put pork chops on the broiling pan and cook it for about 5 minutes or until you see that it is brown from each side.
- Put mayonnaise evenly on French rolls and also put one pork chop on each roll.
- Put chili sauce on the meat and add some lime juice, while topping it with onion, pepper, cucumber, salt and cilantro.
- Add some more lime juice just before serving.

Serving: 4

Timing Information:

Preparation	Cooking	Total Time
10 mins	5 mins	15 mins

Nutritional Information:

Calories	627 kcal
Carbohydrates	72.1 g
Cholesterol	124 mg
Fat	12.1 g
Fiber	3.3 g
Protein	55.3 g
Sodium	1005 mg

* Percent Daily Values are based on a 2,000 calorie diet.

Printed in Great Britain
by Amazon

26386362R00145